BRADNER LIBRARY
SCHOOLCRAFT COLLEGE
18600 HAGGERTY ROAD
LIVONIA, MICHIGAN 48152

SCHOOLCRAFT COLLEGE LIBRARY

3 3013 00132204 3

HQ 799 .I62 A7313 2011
Arefi, Armin.
Green ribbons and turbans

RAWN

W9-DGV-129

GREEN RIBBONS AND TURBANS

YOUNG IRANIANS AGAINST THE MULLAHS

ARMIN AREFI

Translated by
JOANNA OSEMAN

ARCADE PUBLISHING
New York

Copyright © Éditions Denoël, 2011

All Rights Reserved. No part of this book may be reproduced in any manner without the express written consent of the publisher, except in the case of brief excerpts in critical reviews or articles. All inquiries should be addressed to Arcade Publishing, 307 West 36th Street, 11th Floor, New York, NY 10018.

Arcade Publishing books may be purchased in bulk at special discounts for sales promotion, corporate gifts, fund-raising, or educational purposes. Special editions can also be created to specifications. For details, contact the Special Sales Department, Arcade Publishing, 307 West 36th Street, 11th Floor, New York, NY 10018 or info@skyhorsepublishing.com.

Arcade Publishing® is a registered trademark of Skyhorse Publishing, Inc.®, a Delaware corporation.

Visit our website at www.arcadepub.com.

10 9 8 7 6 5 4 3 2 1

Jacket design by Adam Bozarth
Cover Photo © Amir Sadeghi

Library of Congress Cataloging-in-Publication Data is available on file.

ISBN: 978-1-61145-319-5

Printed in the United States of America

1

"*O*H, PRETTY GIRL FROM IRAN! *I wanna be your man!*" As the song's bass line kicks in in this North Tehran apartment, a Persian bombshell makes her entrance. Nose job, bleached hair, and no shortage of makeup, she stares hungrily at the men in her midst. Meet Helya, twenty-two years old. Her black headscarf safely tucked away in the closet, she emerges from the bathroom in a lace teddy and a micromini that barely reaches the tops of her legs. On the other side of the room, twenty-four-year-old Omid, his black shirt unbuttoned and gelled hair styled for the occasion, takes one last shot of *Aragh Sagi* (a local, home-distilled liquor). Tonight's festivities, a party to mark the twenty-fifth birthday of the wealthy hostess, Hala, are taking place in Fereshteh, a high-end neighborhood of the Iranian capital. As proof of invitation to the event, each guest must whisper the password "Islam is in danger" into the intercom before gaining admission. The number of guests has been kept to a minimum and all belong to Tehran's rich bourgeoisie.

It is party time. Bass thumping, furniture shaking, the guests scream along with the music. "Ahaii. Ahaii. Jooooon."

"Oh, pretty lady, with your arched eyebrows and sweet, honey eyes," a deep, soothing voice ripples across the room. Omid approaches the beautiful Helya. She turns her back on him, pretending not to have noticed his presence, and the game is on. "*I wanna come to your front door,*" the singer continues. Omid circles the young woman, shaking his hips like a pro but being sure not to touch her.

"*That's not what I want,*" comes the female singer's shrill reply. As for Helya, she smiles faintly and disappears backward through the crowd, waving her arms as if they were tentacles.

"*I'm gonna talk to your father . . .*" The young man draws closer to his prey, who in turn pouts her scarlet lips, making herself even more desirable.

"*But that's not what I want . . .*" All of a sudden, she turns on her heels, and Omid finds himself trapped in her arms.

"*I'm gonna tell him I'm in love with his daughter . . .*" The two young dancers become one as they move to the beat of the latest Iranian pop hit, made in Los Angeles and forbidden within the Islamic Republic.

"*I want to marry you . . .*"

A few seconds later, the door to the adjacent bedroom slams shut. The couple has disappeared and a dozen others will later follow in their footsteps. In the living room stands a large table where chips, yogurt, and salad Olivier (a mayonnaise-based savory mix of egg and potato) accompany bottles of Jack Daniel's, Smirnoff ($70 apiece), and Bacardi (Islam really is in danger). Access to the kitchen is obstructed by a long line which snakes right out into the living room. Perhaps to try the delicious *ghormeh sabzi* (a lamb stew served with rice) which is simmering away on the stove top? Not quite: On the countertop, rather, are three long lines of cocaine, which each patient guest will sample in turn. For those who are not interested in this particular treat, the next room along is the ecstasy den. The result of this is a group of four wide-eyed young men who, since sometime earlier, have been talking at alarming speed, planning a dramatic escape from Iran by jumping from the window. At the other end of the large front room, another group sits crashed out around an opium-filled hookah pipe.

The bedroom door reopens and Omid rejoins the crowd, barely taking the time to fix his jeans. "Welcome to the Islamic Republic," he laughs. "Paradise on earth, as long as you can afford it." Omid forces a smile, for he himself—a student from Tehran—was far from born with a silver spoon in his mouth. He owes his invitation to this dream party to Morteza, a rich friend. Luckily for him, his real identity remains a secret, or he would never have had the slightest chance of hooking up with the beautiful Helya; even the evening's delights, however, cannot cover up his deep depression. His financial situation is dire—he comes from a middle-class family and is still in school—and he still has to complete two years of military service, meaning that he is forced to remain in the Islamic Republic. This is not the case for most of the young people here tonight. Within a few weeks, a month, or perhaps a year at most, they will all have left the country for the United States, Canada, or Europe, and all thanks to Mom and Dad's bank account.

"We're sick of this president, of this country. *Get out if you can* is this summer's big hit," Helya laughs. And with that, the beautiful Iranian woman has hit the nail on the head: Since Ahmadinejad's election in 2005, her country has become a hell on earth.

"Ahmadinejad has ruined everything in his path. Everything," Omid sighs. "You can't even walk down the street without someone giving you a hard time for the way you dress. My university has been Islamized. Our most prominent professors have been laid off, our best politically active students have been kicked out, the image of our country overseas has been dragged through the mud. It's like being back in the first few hours of the revolution." He downs another shot of *Aragh Sagi*. The pleasures of the moment are what keep this young man alive.

"Everyone is depressed, and the only thing we can do is to escape it in any way possible. Our parents have seen another way of life but not us; we've only ever lived under the Islamic Republic. We're really a wasted generation." He takes a big hit of opium. He may not be a fan of this regime, but the young man knows full well that it will not fall as easily as all that. "Here you can screw, drink, take drugs. But so much as stick your little finger into anything to do with politics, and you disappear."

If these young people are so vehemently opposed to the regime, then why are they not at least *talking* about another revolution? The student knows exactly where he stands on that one. "My parents already had a revolution, and we all know what the result of that was. The country has taken a leap back a hundred years in just thirty." A month away from the presidential election, he is under no illusions.

"Everything's fixed in advance anyway. The vast majority of candidates have been eliminated. Those that remain have been handpicked by the regime and will help to keep it alive," he explains, going on to warn against having too much faith in the so-called "reformists," who themselves are far from what you would call democratic.

"Mousavi's great hope?" he bursts out laughing. "When Mousavi was prime minister, over eight thousand opponents of the regime were executed. Have you forgotten that? He's from the same mold as Ahmadinejad." In 2001, he voted for the reformist Khatami and his promises of freedom. "I'm still kicking myself for that to this day. He betrayed us, offered us only superficial freedom, and just prolonged our suffering by eight years. I'll never vote again."

All of a sudden, the intercom buzzes. "Police. Open this door."

Cries all around as girls and guys are pushed toward separate bedrooms before the officers arrive: a lost cause, given that many of the guests are simply too high to understand what is going on. Now there is knocking at the door.

"Open up, that's an order."

Gripped by fear, the party's hostess opens the door. Unfortunately for her, it is not really the police but, far more serious, four Basiji militiamen in green uniforms. In silence they look at each guest with disgust, focusing in particular on the girls and their outfits, before shouting, "Whores . . . infidels . . . what is going on in here?" Apparently, this is the first time they have attended an event quite like this one.

Amir, one of the young men present that evening, tries to calm things down. The youngest Basiji walks up to him, sniffs at him, and out of nowhere, punches him hard in the face. Terror sets in. Amir, paralyzed by fear despite his far superior size and build, remains stoic. The militiamen charge at the table, smashing all of the alcohol bottles as the guests begin to tremble.

"You're going to pay for this; you're really going to pay." The young militiaman is not wrong. Ten minutes later and they are gone, but not empty-handed. No need to worry about Amir; they chose not to take him away with them this time, opting rather for a pile of traveler's checks, worth a grand total of two million tomans (almost $3,000).

"Bunch of *oghdéi* [assholes]," cries Hala.

"Fucking Islamic Republic," Omid is furious.

Things could have been worse, but the apartment is trashed. The party is definitely over.

2

NORTH TEHRAN'S NIGHTTIME ADVENTURES behind us, the narrow streets lay deserted under the beating sun. There are no miniskirts to be seen here, just a few black chadors wandering about, eventually disappearing into small shacks. It is midday, a solemn voice rings out from the neighborhood mosque, and an old blind man plays santoor on the sidewalk. A little farther down, a group of shopkeepers are chatting outside their stores, running their fingers over their rosaries. We are in Shoush, a working-class neighborhood in the south of the Iranian capital. Twenty-two-year-old Javad, sporting a three-day beard, Palestinian keffiyeh, and tucked-in shirt, is going from door to door with posters and pamphlets for Mahmoud Ahmadinejad.

"I am your humble servant," the young man announces as each door is opened. Javad grew up in this neighborhood. His father died during the Iran-Iraq war, at which point it fell to him to take the reigns as head of the family. There is no point in asking him about any qualifications he may have; the answer is none. In a country that judges people on either social standing or education level, Javad simply does not count.

Religion has always held a special place in the boy's heart. It was in the name of Islam that his father took part in the revolution thirty years ago, and the faith and admiration he held for Imam Khomeini led him to make the ultimate sacrifice on the front line in 1987.

"It would have been an honor to blow myself up in front of an enemy tank, like the young martyr Hossein Fahmideh," Javad says with regret. "But I was too young."

This culture of martyrdom is the only way of life the boy has ever known, and hand in hand with that comes the hatred of a single enemy: The West and its decadence. "It was the West that backed the Shah's dictatorship against the Iranian people and then forged an eight-year alliance with Saddam Hussein against us, providing him with chemical weapons. As if that weren't enough, they then threw the Palestinians out of their own country and invaded Iraq and Afghanistan. And you want to talk to me about democracy?"

It should be pointed out that Javad spent his childhood watching the five state television stations and that he rejects both satellite television and its "perverted programming,"—watched secretly in almost all Iranian homes—and the Internet. The young man does not even have an email address.

He has been attending the local mosque since he was a teenager. There he finds guidance and comfort and claims never to miss a single of the five obligatory daily prayers. On his fifteenth birthday, something that he will never forget led him to turn a corner in his life.

"The mosque imam asked to speak to me in private. He treated me like a grown man and offered to pay my family back for all the sacrifices they had made since the Islamic Revolution."

That is putting it mildly. What the imam had to offer was a monthly stipend of $415 dollars, to be paid on top of the $275 the family had already been receiving each month since his father's death. And what did he ask in return? That the boy become a Basiji.

The Basij ("mobilized" in Persian) is a paramilitary force which was formed by Ayatollah Khomeini and made up of young volunteers whose mission it was to back up Islamic Republic troops on the front lines of the Iran-Iraq war. The militiamen's task today, however, is another thing altogether.

"The imam asked me to maintain order and morals among my peers, throughout my neighborhood, but also among the rich of North Tehran." In particular, his targets are the children of the capital's affluent families, a generation of "spoilt traitors" that Javad curses and insults on a daily basis. On top of the considerable wage (the average salary in Iran is $415), he is given a green uniform and, most important of all, weapons. Thanks to the latter, this little kid has become someone to respect in his neighborhood, and there is sure to be trouble if you fail to show him enough of it.

For the last few months, Javad's sole mission has been to prevent Western culture from invading his country. "They're trying to make Islam disappear and to force our sisters out of their chadors through their Zionist-backed programs. But, thanks to me and others like me, their plans are doomed to failure."

The young man does not hesitate to resort to using force with his fellow countrymen—mostly in the form of a good punch or two—if it means reaching his goal. For almost a year now he has stepped up security patrols in the north of the capital to "encourage" his sisters, *and* also his brothers, to respect Islamic dress code.

"Westerners are trying to export their homosexuals and their prostitutes. We won't stand for it." These days, when Javad walks in the street, it is with a certain swagger. People respect him; some even run from him. He would not give up this power, which fell from above like a divine blessing, for anything in the world. So if beating people is what he has to do, particularly the "spoilt degenerates," as he likes to call them, then beat them up he will.

Javad has never been out with a girl, at least not officially. He has charged his mother with the task of finding him a *najib* (clean) wife, who has never known a man up close or even from afar ("who has seen neither sunlight nor moonlight," as the Persian saying has it). In secret, he dreams of the day that he himself will die like his father, a martyr to Ayatollah Khamenei, supreme leader of the Islamic Republic, an honor through which he will gain access to heaven and the seventy sublime virgins who await him there, a tale repeated to him since his early childhood.

It is for these reasons that Javad is calling for people to vote for Mahmoud Ahmadinejad, the only candidate able to enforce the values that he holds so dear. This is what he believes, and is certainly the opinion of the neighborhood imam, who repeats it at any chance he gets.

"For four years, our president has taken care of us, the working class, like nobody else before him. He redistributed oil money among us; he didn't send it overseas. He has raised Iran's prestige around the world by standing up to the enemy, particularly on the nuclear issue, and he has put his trust in us by asking that we deal with girls who do not wear the veil correctly, who confuse sidewalk with catwalk. What else can I say? He's a real gentleman."

So it is that the young man is willing to do everything in his power to prevent another candidate from winning, in particular one of the reformists, Mousavi and Karoubi.

"These foreign agents pose a serious threat to Islam. Khatami's two terms in office[1] brought nothing but corruption, prostitution, and Western influence to the heart of our country. It is out of the question that such a thing should ever happen again."

A woman in a black chador suddenly crosses the street in front of him. Embarrassed, Javad lowers his gaze and makes sure that their eyes do not meet. "There is equality here. It is my job not to look at them so that they may not tempt me. As for them, their job is to dress appropriately. It's as simple as that."

In every house, Javad praises his president, the self-proclaimed "nation's street sweeper," and in every house he is welcomed, respected, and offered tea. There is not one person who would dare to shut the door in his face. A month away from the presidential election, the young Basiji still has many families to convince, but given that he knows everyone in this neighborhood, and that everything that goes on here is public knowledge, they would be well advised to tow the line.

3

"We're finally going to see the back of him." Holed up in a room in this six-floor apartment building in the west of Tehran, twenty-seven-year-old Arya adds the finishing touches to *90 Minutes of Politics*, a CD he is soon to put into distribution. Its title is a reference to the popular Iranian soccer show *90 Minutes*, and in two forty-five-minute documentaries, a group of young reformists dissect the last four years of rule under the ultraconservative president. "We're going to ruin him," he exclaims with a grin.

The official campaign season for this tenth presidential election began on 2 khordad 1388 (May 23, 2009), and this date saw over twenty thousand people descend upon Azadi, an indoor stadium with only twelve thousand seats. The reason for this gathering was a rally to mark the candidature of reformist Mir-Hossein Mousavi, President Ahmadinejad's main rival. The young Iranians present are not even old enough to remember his time as prime minister, and after his eight years at the head of the government, he disappeared from politics (much like a certain Lionel[1]). So just how has he managed to rally so many supporters?

"They have been behind him ever since Khatami, our reformist ex-president, made his speech. He too should have put himself forward for the election, but he was prevented from doing so. Supreme leader Ayatollah Khamenei asked Khatami, off the record, to withdraw his candidature. You want to know why? Because he knew just how popular he still was in Iran. This is not the case for Mousavi, who is the supreme leader's archenemy, and he feels sure that not only will he lose the election, but that he will be wiped from the political spectrum once and for all," Arya explains.

During Mousavi's time as prime minister, Khamenei himself was the president of the republic. Their respective followers clashed continuously until Khamenei became leader and eliminated the post of prime minister.

Before teaming up with the reformist candidate, Arya worked as a journalist for a large reformist newspaper. After the paper was closed down by Mahmoud Ahmadinejad in 2008, he began writing for several of the reformist Internet sites that were beginning to spring up on the web. Working on his thesis at the prestigious University of Tehran, he was named as one of the Mousavi campaign's student leaders.

Being a reformer, however, is not easy in the Islamic Republic. There was an eight-year period during which the cause had an opportunity to make some headway, during President Khatami's two terms in office from 1997 to 2005, but the young masses who had turned out to vote for him in such numbers had only become disillusioned with his superficial offers of freedom. Many people blamed him for an outpouring of discontent and believed that his time in office served only to allow the Islamic Republic to sustain itself. This mindset was largely responsible for the large number of voters who boycotted the 2005 presidential election, offering Mahmoud Ahmadinejad his victory on a plate.

"And now they're kicking themselves," Arya explains, "The last four years have shown them just how good they had it under Khatami."

So it is that Ahmadinejad's campaign is not so much being pitched against that of Mousavi but rather against a reminder of Khatami's two terms. Arya has stepped up his trips to the provinces, his meetings, and his articles, through which he compares life under the respective rule of these two men.

"It is not a pretty picture to say the least. Nobody has ever managed to ruin the country in such a short period of time. Ahmadinejad has succeeded in riling everybody."

In order to do their bit in preventing the reelection of this ultraconservative, many Iranians have given over their properties, free of charge, to the Mousavi campaign, the brand-new apartment in which Arya is working today being but one example.

"In terms of culture, people were reading Gabriel García Márquez under Khatami, and they were listening to Metallica and watching Hatamikia movies.[2] Ahmadinejad banned all of these things, and so today they've all been forced underground."

The list of damages is even more alarming when it comes to the press. "I've been unemployed for months now, without any benefits of course. I can't help but laugh when I hear Ahmadinejad bemoaning the criticism of the press. Show me one such occurrence and I swear I'll become an ayatollah."

This environment is hard for him to bear after his experience under Khatami, when he witnessed the birth of many critical, reformist titles. "He woke up the nation by teaching them to read newspapers, and good ones too." Arya, however, has a short memory, as this creation of new newspapers came hand in hand with the closing down of many others.

"Unfortunately, Khatami just didn't have full power at his disposal," he laments. "The Ministry of Culture—which was under his control—was handing out authorizations left, right, and center, but no sooner were they handed out than Saeed Mortazavi, Tehran's ultraconservative prosecutor,[3] would just shut them down one by one." A strange smile creeps across the young man's face. "But we were sneaky. We would just show up again the next day, under a different name, and the ministry just encouraged us, giving us brand-new authorizations every time." A good number of these former reformist ministers now live in forced exile overseas whereas others became the brains behind the Green Movement.

The main criticism of Mousavi and Khatami, especially from international voices, circulates around the murders of regime opponents and intellectuals that took place during their respective terms (tens under Khatami, several thousand under Mousavi).

"Neither Mousavi nor Khatami was directly responsible for these killings as far as I know"—Arya is defensive—"and the system in place in Iran is such that power is not always in the hands of the president of the republic. They weren't even able to investigate these murders."

As well as distributing his CD, Arya devotes his time to passing out posters, leaflets, and speeches by candidate Mousavi. "Green is a color which symbolizes several things," he explains. "It's the color of

Islam, of peace, and of life." Saeed Hajjarian, former advisor to President Khatami and one of the reformist movement's key players, is responsible for the use of this symbol.

Another of Arya's jobs is to promote the reformer over the Internet, particularly via the social networking sites Facebook and Twitter, and this is all able to take place thanks to the generous support of Iran's ex-president, the moderate Hashemi Rafsandjani. Unfortunately though, the latter is seen by many as a symbol of corruption.

"I don't see what the problem is with that," the unemployed journalist is again defensive. "Obama did the same thing during his campaign, announcing that he would welcome any form of financial support. Change requires spending."

As well as Mousavi, there is one other serious hopeful standing against the incumbent president: the seventy-year-old Mehdi Karoubi, former chairman of the Iranian parliament who came third in the 2005 presidential election. Complaining (even back then) of mass fraud and its role in Ahmadinejad's victory, he resigned from all of his political posts and formed the National Trust party and a newspaper of the same name. Today he makes a perfect third option between reformists and conservatives, but Arya does not trust him one bit.

"As chairman of one of the most reformist parliaments the Islamic Republic has ever seen, he did everything in his power to halt its activities, to such an extent that many of its strongest representatives resigned. Everyone but him."

Enough of all of these rumors and scandals; the young man's priority today is to get rid of the ultraconservative. The incumbent president has been particularly successful in stirring up two areas, both of which have caused Arya a great deal of personal suffering: foreign policy and the economic management of the country.

"The most important thing for me, whether the regime calls itself the Islamic Republic or some other name, is that Iran, my country, is perceived well around the world. But last year when I, as an Iranian man, traveled to Germany, they took my digital fingerprints the second I arrived at the airport. When I bought things at the supermarket, they checked my bills to see if they were fakes. Why would they do all that?

"Because some 'crazy' guy decides that he's going to launch an attack on something that nobody before has *ever* dared to attack: the Holocaust. When Khatami went before the United Nations, he commanded respect when he talked about dialogue among civilizations. What did Ahmadinejad do? He recited prayers in Arabic, his halo glowing as the seats in front of him emptied, and a red clown nose was thrown at his face."

Arya, so proud of his roots, of Persian civilization and its five-thousand-year history, can no longer hide his feelings. "I'm ashamed. Ashamed of this populist rhetoric. Ashamed to watch him shouting out to his crowd of people supposedly representing the population, 'How long have you been waiting here for me? Since ten o'clock this morning? Eleven o'clock? Twelve o'clock?' And when they cheer him as if he were an idol, everyone forgets that any time he goes *anywhere* new, at least twenty buses are there to transport his 'supporters' from province to province. I'm ashamed when he rebuilds the Jamkaran highway[4] and replaces all of the streetlights in preparation for the arrival of Mahdi.[5] Ashamed when he has the nerve, on live television, to just change the inflation rate in his favor, to reduce it to 13 percent when the central bank has just announced it to be at 25 percent."

Among this collection of failings, though, there is at least one successful measure that can be attributed to the Iranian president: the nuclear program. Arya laughs. "He was so grandiose about the whole thing. He managed to play the West for four years. He never stopped taking more time, delaying things, going back on his word. But all that is dangerous, they're reaching the end of their tether. Why construct long-range missiles with so many warheads? The facts show that you simply can't count on him for anything."

Mousavi, however, has no intention of abandoning the nuclear program either, which begs the question: Can you really put your faith in a reformer who is nonetheless a member of the Islamic regime and whose hands and feet will often be tied? Once again, Arya takes refuge in the case of Ahmadinejad's predecessor, reformist Mohammad Khatami.

"Khatami played an active role and signed every possible treaty you can imagine in order to allow Iran access to civil nuclear energy."

The young reformist insists on this last point, and then takes it one step further. "But the most important thing was that his nonabrasive, amiable politics meant that people were not afraid of Iran, and that's what makes all the difference. It is under Ahmadinejad's rule that we've not only had no less than three UN resolutions but also threats of attack from the Israelis."

For four years the Western press has been painting the picture that the nuclear program is the one subject on which the Iranian regime and the country's population unanimously agree, tying them together as a question of national pride. The young man shakes his head. "It's not the case anymore. People have to think first and foremost of putting bread on the table and that's what has turned them against Ahmadinejad."

On this topic, the prices speak for themselves. "When Khatami was in power, a house in the Saadat Abad neighborhood went for one million tomans per square meter (just over $1,000). Under Ahmadinejad, the price has risen to six million tomans (over $6,000). Under Khatami you could buy meat for five thousand tomans a kilo ($5.15), under Ahmadinejad it is twelve thousand tomans ($12.35). The bread I used to get for twenty-five tomans (3¢) now costs me two hundred (24¢), and the gas that was once eighty tomans a liter (8¢) now costs me four hundred (40¢)."

On top of these figures, it is worth pointing out that Khatami had to make do with an oil export value of approximately forty dollars a barrel while under Ahmadinejad this has risen to eighty dollars. Now, for the first time, Arya turns his attentions to the current reformist candidate for the presidency.

"Mousavi, even in the midst of war, succeeded in running the country when a barrel of oil was worth eight dollars and when the dollar was equal to seven tomans.[6] This was his top accomplishment, and one that begs the question: Where has all the money from Ahmadinejad's budget gone?" In the young man's opinion, the most significant problem with the Iranian economy is the fact that it is entirely state-operated and dependent on oil.

"Privatization has no place in Iran and so competition doesn't exist, which leaves the government to dictate prices. It's just one big racket. This is especially clear when you consider that Ahmadinejad's cabinet is made up entirely of his personal acquaintances and highly underqualified friends, and that he eradicated all of the control systems that could have been of use to him. Worst of all, by refusing to subsidize businesses within the country, Ahmadinejad was responsible for their ruin by opening the Iranian market up to one of his only allies: China. Not to mention the bribes offered to Venezuela, Sudan, Lebanon, and Syria to finance anti-Americanism."

So whatever happened to the self-proclaimed "servant of the Iranian people," the "nation's street sweeper," the Ahmadinejad that promised to bring oil money to the tables of the underprivileged? Arya laughs. "Oh they got the money . . . during the last month of his term. Same goes for pensions, which have just been increased. During his four years in office, Ahmadinejad never went out to the provinces without his book of 50,000 tomans traveler's checks, which he simply handed out down the line. What happens if you send a letter to the president? You get a reply in the form of a 50,000 tomans check. All of this has led to a rise in inflation and has only benefited a small number of people."

Since the beginning of the campaign, Arya has been scouring the parks in the capital's south to look for retirees and young workers. His first question: Why did their salary not go up until the final month of Ahmadinejad's term in office? The answer is final. "Look, it went up. That's what counts. I don't want to go home to my wife and children at the end of the month with nothing in my pockets."

The Iranian journalist lowers his head. "Ahmadinejad has lost a lot of his working-class base because he was simply not able to hand out his checks to the entire country. But nonetheless, he still has his supporters; there are still plenty of 'cows' [fools] out there in this country."

One story in particular caused a stir recently. As well as his famous checks, the Iranian president, over the last few months, has been handing out potatoes in the provinces in order to increase his popularity among voters, to such an extent that on May 23, the first day of the campaign, Mousavi supporters began chanting in the stadium, "We don't want a potato government."

Arya forces a smile. "Unfortunately the biggest curse here isn't even the government. It's the people."

What was that? Can he really say that, when for thirty years the regime has suppressed its population in the name of religion? Arya smiles again. "Because this very population is still rooted to this religion. Whether you like it or not, Iran is a religious, superstitious society, and the regime knows exactly how to play on that. A lot of my friends say that they oppose Islam. They drink alcohol and sleep around, but deep down, if someone insults one of the imams, they can't help but get angry out of a fear of being turned into a cockroach. That's why the only real solution to this is to let society take the time it needs for deep reform. And it will take a while."

Thirty years after the Islamic Revolution, in a country where 70 percent of the seventy-three million inhabitants are young people, yearning for some kind of alternative to this mullahcracy, why are they not talking of another revolution?

"It's out of the question," is Arya's retort. "Our parents had their ideals and could no longer stand to live under the Shah's regime. They had a revolution, and this is the result. Unfortunately, there is no credible alternative to the Islamic Republic in existence today, and you have to remember that whatever the regime in power, the most important thing for me and my peers is to earn a living and survive."

4

On Wednesday, June 3, 2009, over forty-five million Iranians are at home, their eyes glued to the television screen. In a bid to show the world the extent to which the country has moved forward, and to demonstrate the democratic nature of this particular election, the Islamic Republic will hold a series of seven American-style televised presidential debates for the first time in its history. After the infamous Guardian Council of the Constitution eliminated over 99 percent of this year's candidates, only four now remain. In other words, these four hand-picked men are the sons of the regime itself.

Tonight's debate is the one everyone has been waiting for. It will see the incumbent president, Mahmoud Ahmadinejad, whose current record is nothing short of catastrophic, face off against his top challenger, Mir-Hossein Mousavi, absent from the political stage since his stint as prime minister from 1981 to 1989, during the Iran-Iraq war. The debate is set to last one and a half hours.

The program, expected to serve as a mere formality for the populist Ahmadinejad—a master at public speaking—quickly veers off track, exceeding the audience's wildest expectations. This is an evening of democracy, the likes of which the country has never seen.

Relaxed in his chair, his hair parted on one side and his suit loose-fitting, Mahmoud Ahmadinejad begins his spiel. In a composed, articulate tone, he is quick to position himself as the victim.

"Since the Islamic Revolution, no government has been made to suffer as many attacks as mine . . . I have come to forgive my critics, but I will not stand by and watch the people or the people's choices be insulted as well . . . During the last election, my opponent was the beneficiary of support and assistance from both inside and outside the country."

The tone of the debate is set: populism (the incumbent president's trademark) and the denunciation of foreign interference (a great classic in Iranian politics). Glued to their screens, the viewers cannot believe their ears. Attacking former governments is akin to attacking the foundations of the Islamic Republic itself and, until this moment, no one has ever dared to do so.

"The younger generation should remember that I am not facing one single candidate here but three . . . At the beginning of my term of office, Mr. Hashemi sent word to one of the Persian Gulf kings, reassuring him that within six months, this government would fall."

The target here is Ahmadinejad's personal nemesis, Ayatollah Hashemi Rafsandjani, a pillar of the Islamic Republic. President of Iran between 1989 and 1997, he lost to Ahmadinejad in the second round of the 2005 presidential election, thanks to a public image swathed in corruption.

"Today, our people are happy. They are moving towards freedom. They are making a name for themselves in the fields of science, research, politics, and particularly foreign policy . . . Today, Iran's people are the most loved of all peoples."

A quick reminder: after Ahmadinejad's four years as head of state, Iran is on the brink of ruin, both on an economic level with rocketing inflation and unemployment figures and from an international standpoint. The subject of UN sanctions as a result of its nuclear program, the country's image is at an all-time low.

"To believe your words, Mr. Mousavi, is to believe that your dear friends left me with a field full of roses, and that I have turned it to ruin."

It is time now for reformist Mir-Hossein Mousavi, with his professor's glasses, white beard, and dark eyebrows, to speak for the first time. His eyes fixed on his notes, his voice rough and almost unintelligible, he responds calmly to the accusations thrown his way, all the while struggling with a charisma which shrivels in the shadow of his opponent's.

"There are two ways to solve our country's problems. On the one hand, there is adventurism, inconsistency, actions geared solely at creating a heroic, populist persona, and egocentrism." Mousavi points to his rival. "On the other hand, there is a logical, well-researched, realistic, and transparent approach, balanced and in full accordance with the law." This is his plan. "To build a powerful Iran, I believe the second to be the better option." He takes a breath and continues. "I am afraid of what will become of this country under a continuation of the kind of leadership this government has exhibited."

He will now single out Ahmadinejad's populist slogans as being largely responsible for his victory four years ago. "These slogans concerning the future of the world are mere hallucinations. There is nothing to back them up."

Now for a list of Ahmadinejad's accomplishments, which he belittles one by one in front of the television audience. First up is the incumbent president's greatest triumph: diplomacy. "As for foreign policy, you have brought shame on our people, stunted our country's internal development, and caused great concern among other nations . . . You then described the Holocaust as a myth! What myth? Your words made Europe, who had begun to distance itself from Israel following the killings in Gaza, turn straight back round to defend it once more."

"Why thank you, Mr. Mousavi," Mahmoud Ahmadinejad responds, a mocking smile creeping across his face. "I mean that as a friend, for I am very fond of you . . . But you have a short memory, Mr. Mousavi. You seem to have forgotten that you yourself announced that you would send armed forces to stand alongside the Palestinian resistance to fight the occupiers."

He points directly at his opponent as he addresses the presenter. "It was he who said that the Zionist regime should be wiped out." These accusations have never been proven.

"As for the nuclear issue, you know full well that the decisions you made in a bid to keep crisis at bay meant that we had to shut down each and every one of our centers."

Here, Ahmadinejad refers to the 2003 Paris accord, which was signed under the reformist President Khatami. He consented to the additional protocol of the nuclear nonproliferation treaty and to a temporary halt on uranium enrichment as an act of goodwill, an agreement which was quickly undone as Ahmadinejad put enrichment facilities back to work.

"Today, the nuclear issue has worked its way down to tenth place on the priority list. At one time they tried to scare us with their ultimate threat: the Security Council. So we went to the Security Council, and what did they do? They imposed sanctions on us. But what effect did they have then, and what effect will they have today?"

While it may be true that the Iranian regime has not been severely affected by the three rounds of sanctions imposed upon it—largely due to a lack of precise targeting—the country's nuclear program currently holds center stage in international concerns once again. The Islamic Republic could soon be hit with a fourth round of sanctions, this time much tougher, as the United States and France have managed to secure the support of Russia, one of Tehran's key strategic allies.

The incumbent president continues his populist tack as he speaks directly to Mousavi. "For the twenty-seven years that you served as prime minister, during the terms of office of Hashemi and later Khatami, the United States wanted to see you gone. Today, its official stance has changed, as Bush announced at the end of his term and Obama has since reiterated. So tell me, if you will, whose foreign policies have been more successful and whose served only to humiliate us? Whose have ensured our independence and whose offered nothing but concessions and ineffectiveness?"

This is a sly move on Ahmadinejad's part, knowing, as he does, just how sensitive Iranians are to even a hint of humiliation in the eyes of the outside world. But what he says is not entirely false, for his violent diatribes have turned the Islamic Republic into a problem that simply cannot be ignored within the region, and have forced President Obama to reach out America's hand to Iranian leaders for the first time in thirty years.

Feeling confident, the ultraconservative president turns the heat up a notch, addressing the other issue which set sparks off around the world (with the exception of some parts of the Arab world): his Holocaust denial.

"I raised two questions about the Holocaust. Two questions, and all of a sudden it is as if I were questioning human rights and history itself. I am deeply shocked. Israel is upset, Europe is upset, and people even dare to say that Iran has been disgraced . . . Today, you too blame me for speaking about the Holocaust. But tell me, why shouldn't we? Should we just sit around and wait for Europe to instruct us on human rights? Or is it up to us to tell them that it is not their place to do so?"

Then comes the icing on the cake; a hint of the propaganda jargon for which he is known. "One must not wait until the enemy turns up on one's doorstep before going to confront him. Today, all threats to Iran have been retracted, once and for all . . . Today, the world stands behind Iran." A difficult statement to get behind when you consider the current threat of an Israeli attack on Iranian nuclear sites, as well as the potential fourth round of UN sanctions.

Mousavi, collected as always, attempts to defend himself, fumbling with his words and being rather overliberal with the colloquial expression *chiz* (thing). Nonetheless, he finally manages to express himself. "As for the Israel issue, we all agree that those living on Palestinian soil, including the people that emigrated there, should get together—be they Jews, Muslims, or Christians—and vote for their future."

He comes now to the moral of the story. "In all matters, if you go too far on one side, you will be forced to go too far on the other. They [Ahmadinejad's government] speak of Israel in this provocative manner, and then they speak of the Holocaust, without any thought as to the long-term consequences of their actions. But the result is that when the situation begins to escalate, along comes one of our representatives to declare to the world that we are, in fact, *friends* of the people of Israel![1] And [Mahmoud Ahmadinejad] allows this man to remain in his position. How can this nation, these thieves, they who have stolen Palestinian territory, suddenly become our friends?"

Then, speaking directly to the Iranian people, Mousavi continues. "Our nation suffers the consequences of these policies on many levels, in terms of its mental well-being, its economic situation, the materials it needs in order to support its industries, its relationship with other countries, the loss in value of its people's passports in the eyes of the rest of the world, and its humiliation across the entire planet."

This distressing list hits home with the many Iranians who have suffered all of these things in just four years. Almost anyone who was able to, particularly among the younger generation, has fled the country. The former prime minister is on a roll.

"To what extent should government take responsibility for the Iranian self-image?" Mousavi hones in on the extreme national pride felt by many Iranians, placing it on a pedestal above Islam, which has been crammed down so many throats by his opponent. He looks, for the first time, as though he might lose his temper.

"The government could not care less about pain and worries of the people," he continues. "I, personally, am sick with worry for them after everything you have put them through."

Mousavi moves now to defend his closest allies, former Presidents Hashemi Rafsandjani and Khatami. "These are not figures to be ignored. Why not invite them, too, to discuss things around the table? But of course, *mashallah* [congratulations], our radio and television services are at the disposal of our friends here.[2] What do they care about me and my ideas?"

This is a first for the Islamic Republic. Applause thunders in living rooms across the nation as Mousavi dares to denounce the Iranian media's bias toward the president.

"What are we putting them through, our students, our youth, our people? Everywhere I go, I listen to their complaints. Some say they were verbally insulted, I hear that you did such and such a thing to one 'star' student[3] arrested another, and expelled a third from his university. All this has created an atmosphere of great pessimism which surrounds this regime . . . sorry, this *government*. No one can be pessimistic about the regime."

This is a huge lapse on Mousavi's part as instead of criticizing Ahmadinejad's government, he accidentally criticizes the Islamic Republic itself. Could this be a telltale lapse? He goes on.

"Has the government ever really taken the time to consider why its relationship with the clergy has deteriorated so? Why its relationship with our intellectuals is no more? Why it has lost its connection to the youth of our nation?"

Ahmadinejad displays a beaming, mocking smile and replies. "Mr. Mousavi, sometimes I feel very sorry for you. Your information is based on ignorance. Mr. Mousavi, during your eight years as prime minister, there was only one single newspaper, a daily paper which published an economic report once a week. What did you do to that newspaper? How many times did you yourself speak out against it? Let me show you something." He lays a series of sheets out on the table.

"Here is a list of newspapers that have insulted my government. In your speech, you are trying to make me out to be a dictator, but I have tolerated these insults. Is that dictatorship? What dictatorship are you talking about? . . . I tolerate my opponents. During my term, there have been over three hundred and twenty such offensive publications. We have not shut down a single newspaper, we have not issued any threats, we have not exerted even the slightest bit of pressure. They continue to write and, with your support, their comments about us are worse than ever."

Could it be that Mahmoud Ahmadinejad has had some kind of memory loss? The majority of reformist publications have seen themselves outlawed under his rule, which has seen the greatest censorship of the press since the advent of the Islamic Revolution.

The debate is becoming childish; the boxing match is about to start, and today there will be no holds barred. The defending champion, Ahmadinejad, throws the first punch.

"You have accused the government of lawlessness. Listen, I do not wish to delve into the details of the ninety-five million tomans which were withdrawn from the Central Bank, without the approval of Parliament, during one summer recess when your government was in power." The pettiness continues. "I, personally, would prefer to discuss this issue of university titles. You have often qualified Mr. Khatami as 'doctor.' You know full well that, in accordance with our laws, you can only call someone a doctor if he holds an official university doctorate. All he has is a bachelor's degree in philosophy."

Ahmadinejad strikes below the belt as he places a further sheet of paper on the table with a sly tone and threatening glance. Whispering, he asks, "Perhaps I could talk to you about this woman's dossier? Her academic dossier? May I?"

The challenger Mousavi responds warily, "Please, be my guest."

The presenter, however, puts a swift end to this intimidation tactic and passes the microphone back to the reformist candidate who, keeping his cool, continues without even a glance in his opponent's direction.

"One of my biggest concerns, and one of this country's major problems, is exactly what we have just witnessed: the fabrication of false documents and a constant tone of accusation to avoid the real issue at stake. In this instance, the issue is that our nation's interior minister claimed to have a PhD while our own president himself was 'completely unaware' of the inferior diploma he actually held. Either the cause of this is a tremendous lack of information, or the cause is something altogether different, something I dare not even think about."

Mousavi is referring here to Interior Minister Ali Kordan, who claimed to have been awarded a PhD from Oxford but was proven to be in possession of no such thing. The reformer moves now to attack the negative impact that the incumbent president's government has had on internal politics or, in other words, his catastrophic management of the economy.

"I have substantial proof that the government has broken the law not once, not twice, but over and over again, and I find this terrifying . . . I do not wish to say that Mr. Ahmadinejad tries consciously to be a dictator, but let's imagine a government that over eight years in power says, 'I do not like this law or that law, this one is not in the country's interest, that one will prevent me from carrying out my plan of action.' What is left of such a country after eight years?"

Mousavi is trying to frighten people by offering this glimpse of the potential outcomes of Ahmadinejad's reelection. "If you remove one law, you must replace it with another, and this must be approved by Parliament."

The reformer looks directly at the camera and raises his voice, quoting concrete figures for the first time tonight. "I want people to understand that one of the main causes of our 25 percent inflation rate is that the Monetary and Credit Council, put in place to limit you as well as me, was removed. Another reason is that the government wishes to be in complete control of all banks and organizations. And that no one intervenes . . . The result: the economic situation that everyone is complaining about."

He counts on his fingers. "Industry has slumped, inflation has reached 25 percent, everybody is unhappy. That is the result of all of this. The money supply has risen to 2.5 times the amount it was at the beginning of your term, the public budget has been allocated illegally, the Management and Planning Organization, whose job it was to prevent you from spending as you saw fit, has been dissolved."

Obviously offended by the liberties taken by his opponent, Ahmadinejad cannot seem to stop grinning while Mousavi, sober as ever, does not flinch as he continues. "I think that our 'friends' here, rather than fabricating false documents, rather than wasting their time on such things, should set about resolving the country's problems, and in so doing, saving it from the crisis that is currently suffocating it."

Mousavi looks once more into the camera and speaks directly to the audience with a stern voice. "In all honesty, one of my main motivations for entering this election is this need to see the law respected . . . I want the people to know that this government . . . when it sees fit, defies laws that were adopted by our own parliament, not to mention the fact that this same parliament is made up primarily of people who support the president anyway."

It is now the reformist candidate's turn to point a finger at this opponent. Mousavi has once more rocked the foundations of the Islamic Republic, having just accused the Iranian parliament of siding with the president on every matter.

The presenter informs Mousavi that his ten minutes are up.[4] He accepts without protest, watching while Ahmadinejad childishly complains, demanding more time to talk. "This debate should be extended to three or four hours . . . I am only given forty-five minutes, with no recognition of the fact that this is three people against one. But that's OK . . ."

In the face of such accusations, the incumbent president kicks back with his favorite surprise attack. "Tell me again, where do Mr. Hashemi's children get their money from? And tell me, which of my ministers has become a billionaire during his term? Which one has stolen money? Which one has acquired property?"

Ahmadinejad once again employs his populist tactics by going after an easy target: former President Hashemi Rafsandjani. One of the Mousavi campaign's financial backers but considered by many to be corrupt, he is despised by a good portion of the Iranian population. Ten years ago, however, anyone making accusations such as these would have ended up in jail.

Ahmadinejad now lays a collection of papers onto the table, announcing them as property deeds. "Who was it that benefited from these property transfers? Your supporters, that's who. And where are the funds for your expensive campaign coming from? Mr. Mousavi, I like you a lot. But how can you be spending so much money? Where is all the money coming from?"

He has still not finished. "Four hundred hectares of land were taken while the people cannot even afford to buy two hectares, an area which would allow four kids to get back to work. Now *that* is lawlessness, Mr. Mousavi. Statoil: that is what we call lawlessness. And, of course, it is Hashemi's son who we find at the root of this story. Lawlessness surrounds the son of one of your backers."

Ahmadinejad is referring here to the scandal which erupted when the oil company Statoil acquired lucrative rights to Iranian oil resources during the presidency of the reformist Khatami, thanks to bribes received by the son of the influential Hashemi Rafsandjani. There was a similar case involving the French giant, Total.

"Mr. Mousavi, when has my government ever said that it did not accept the law? I doubt that you can come up with one single case."

The ultraconservative president grabs a piece of paper, brandishing it at the camera. Resuming his threatening tone and screwing up his eyes as he speaks, he addresses his opponent once more.

"I have, in my hand, the dossier of a woman who you know very well. She sits by your side throughout your election campaign. Violating all laws during her time as a government employee, she studied for two master's degrees."

Mousavi stays calm, as he has done throughout this debate.

"She earned her doctorate without passing the national exam and went on to teach in a subject which was not her specialty. Without having the correct qualifications, she was appointed dean of a university. Now *that* is lawlessness."

Mousavi closes his eyes in silence.

"And I do not support this kind of thing. Our government respects the law. I do not have the figures on me, but I know that in this same term, during which you claim the economy has suffered, our country's economic situation has been far superior to that of former governments. It has been simply *wonderful* next to yours."

During this time Mousavi, avoiding eye contact, takes notes, waiting for his turn to speak. For the first time, a smile creeps across the reformist's face.

"Certain issues have been raised here that leave me in a position of not knowing how to respond." He now gets his chance. "One of the problems of debating with Mr. Ahmadinejad is that unusual questions are often raised."

Ahmadinejad interjects, grumbling, "You accuse me of lawlessness . . ."

"Don't interrupt me," Mousavi replies firmly. "Look at how you behave on state media, on Internet sites. We all know who is behind them and how they operate."

The Islamic Republic finds itself in the line of fire once again, this time with the questioning of its media partiality. Mousavi takes a turn at attacking his opponent, whose permanent smile belies his awkwardness.

"It is my turn to speak," he continues, looking directly at the camera and not once at his rival. His first job is to respond to the accusations thrown at his campaign treasurer, Rafsandjani.

"Without wishing to speak for them, I believe they will be justified in being upset at your words. Perhaps our viewers tonight will also be unhappy at seeing the president of their republic accuse a citizen, his family, and his children in front of at least fifty million people when he is not even on the stage to defend himself."

Mahmoud Ahmadinejad's biggest obstacle to his reelection speaks to the people directly through the camera. "We welcome the support of anyone who offers it . . . But unlike certain of our friends here, we do not grasp at every opportunity that comes our way to manipulate and exploit the government and its offices, including the Ministry of Interior and state television." He raises his fist. "As for us, we welcome any person who wishes to support me in my bid to take back the vote and enact real change. That is my wish."

His eyes wide, he lets loose for the first time. "To everybody out there who wants to see an end to this kind of atmosphere, where people find themselves so easily condemned . . ." The challenger raises the tone as he points to Ahmadinejad. "This man before me holds up a photo of my wife"—he mimics Ahmadinejad brandishing his wife's resume at the camera—"and declares, 'She did this, she did that.' This person is one of the greatest intellectual women in this country, she worked for ten years to earn her PhD in political science, and is proud to have also earned a master of arts and proud of her position as a Quran scholar. The proof of this—the relevant documentation—exists, and I am sure that she will produce them immediately. Sites that are closely tied to you have created much negativity in her regard."

Here Mousavi scores points with the Iranian television audience for his display of *gheyrat*, or honor. By standing up to a man who shows a lack of respect towards his wife in his presence, this husband counterattacks in style.

"I have information in my possession to the unfortunate effect that—and this is one of the problems with this government—a number of executive advisors working for the president of the republic have chosen not to try to solve the problems of the people, but rather to spend their time going through files in an attempt to dredge up something with which to attack another tonight." His stern expression cuts through the lens like a knife. "I am here to change this way of thinking. I am here to tell the people that I will put a stop to this mentality." Why stop when you are on a roll? "Mr. Ahmadinejad has stated that the star system was created during Mr. Moein's[5] tenure. If this is true, then it was a grave mistake on his part. But one thing I am sure of is that during his time, they never attacked or arrested people in this same manner."

Mahmoud Ahmadinejad, laughing, interrupts his opponent once more. "You must excuse me, Mr. Mousavi . . ."

But his challenger is not about to be easily defeated and continues his role as director of operations, all the while mocking his rival as best he can.

"You must not encroach upon my time to speak."

Turning back to the camera, he continues. "Look, what we want is to act in conjunction with the law."

Ahmadinejad lets out a strange moan, which Mousavi ignores. "These policies are reminiscent of the Qadjar era, during which governors had a treasury that they could dip into at will and from which they could distribute money left, right, and center."

He now deals his final punch. "This inflation, this unemployment, this addiction, and this cultural demise are all a result of these policies." He raises his voice. "The same goes for our foreign policy failings, and the fact that we do not have a single ally in the region . . . You repeat over and over again that America will fall. For four years we have been hearing that Israel is on the point of being wiped out, that France, that America . . ." He mocks Ahmadinejad, mimicking his gestures. "We have built our diplomacy around this notion, and it is clear that we have gone astray, that we have made some serious mistakes.

"All of these things have caused our country harm—harm we have suffered for four years, the level of which is of immense proportions." Again, he looks into the camera. "This is what has led me to stand in these elections." He concludes, "I address this message to the people: I am one of you and I have come home to you now.[6] The people will decide; they will be the judges of Mr. Ahmadinejad's term. They will see for themselves the methods and policies which have been employed, and the final decision is in their hands. I felt, personally, that our country was in danger and that it was my duty to step forward. I thank the people, I know what they are made of, and I ask them to look closely, to pay close attention to their values."

This final statement is an important one, as Mousavi reminds the people to look beyond the superficial as they failed to do when they so quickly swallowed up Ahmadinejad's populist speeches four years earlier.

The time has come for the knockout blow, with Mousavi dishing up a few deadly examples. "To humiliate your people by dragging them along behind a car, all to make it look like yours is the politics of the people, is not the way to do things." He refers here to one example of Ahmadinejad's numerous, sensationalized trips to the provinces during which a great crowd of his followers chased his car.

"What the people need is job creation, stronger national production, and increased industry. They do not need to see imported basmati invading the rice paddies of Rasht, for their tea to be shipped in from overseas. I went to Hamedan and it's strange, but their local specialty is garlic. They say now that Chinese garlic has come onto the scene, they can no longer grow their own. These kinds of things must end."

Mousavi has hit a raw nerve: China, one of Tehran's only remaining powerful allies, has bombarded the Iranian market, ruining a great number of national industries. "We must have at least some pride as far as Iran's economy is concerned," he summarizes.

Now for one last master stroke, for which Mousavi plays with the thousand-year-old nationalism of the Iranian people. "I find it humiliating that our industry, our agriculture, our production, our economy, and our culture are exposed to this level of destruction, and I hope that the results of this debate, of this conversation, *inshallah*, will come out in favor of our great Islamic Revolution, *inshallah*."

That sums it up: Mousavi is a "reformer" and would do nothing that would threaten the Iranian regime, the Islamic Republic.

Thrown off guard for the first time, it seems as though Ahmadinejad has something else to say, but his time is up. After the presenter bids the viewers good night and the cameras pan out from the two candidates, Ahmadinejad moans.

"Mr. Mousavi makes accusations one after another and then says that he does not wish to talk. How interesting . . ." His voice fades away and he is replaced by a commercial.

Tonight's debate is over. The Iranian television audience has been spoiled with this historic first; in barely an hour and a half, thirty years of the Islamic Republic have been picked apart as Mahmoud Ahmadinejad and Mir-Hossein Mousavi battled it out in a fratricidal war. More importantly, the millions of Iranians beaten down by four nightmare years rejoiced at every exchange, found hope, and began, for the first time, to believe in the defeat of the ultraconservative. The latter, expected to come out on top, has been ridiculed by his opponent. He may have managed to draw a few underprivileged and misinformed families to his side, thanks to a handful of provocative statements whose sources he will never reveal. But one thing is for certain: if the Islamic Republic lost tonight in terms of prestige and legitimacy, it can also be said to have claimed a noteworthy victory. Given that Iranians are essentially *jav guir*—in other words, strongly influenced by their emotions—there should be one hell of a crowd next week outside the polling stations.

5

*I*T IS ONE O'CLOCK in the morning and Omid, sleeping peacefully after an evening of bouncing around in front of the television, is awoken by the telephone. It is his best friend, Hamid, in a fit of excitement.

"Get your butt down here. Valiasr, man, quick as you can . . . it's party time!"

Not quite sure whether or not he is still dreaming, Omid pulls on his clothes, jumps in the car, and heads over to Tehran's main city street to see what all the fuss is about. En route, he is surprised to see that, despite the late hour, there is still light coming from many of the city's windows, and from the streets around him comes a cacophony of car horns. Did Iran win the World Cup or something? Omid parks in an adjacent street and goes the rest of the way on foot. As he finally turns into his destination, a surprising scene greets him: Valiasr is teeming with people, a giant human traffic jam for the poor vehicles trying to get through.

"By the end of the week, Ahmadi will be gone," comes the cry from hundreds of Iranians, wrists adorned with green ribbons. Ecstatic drivers honk their horns in rhythm, providing a deafening accompaniment to the crowd's chants.

"*Dameshoon garm* [literally, 'May your breath be warm,' or 'Bravo'],"
Omid screams. "You wouldn't see a scene like this anywhere but Iran."
The young man finally catches up with his friend Hamid, who himself had been called by a different friend to come down.

"It's crazy down here, and the cops are letting us do whatever we want," he had insisted on the phone.

Tonight, the Iranian women around them are dressed to the nines. It is like being at a fashion show, or perhaps more accurately, a car show, going by the parade of vehicles decked out in banners, posters, ribbons, and green stickers in effigy of Mir-Hossein Mousavi. Inside, dark makeup has been applied to extremes, and loose headscarves reveal bleached blond hair whose owners boast nose jobs (a sign of wealth) and, the icing on the cake, fingernails that have been painted green. Omid is hovering by the open window which currently separates him from two such beautiful creatures.

"Oh, my love . . . my angel. Swear that if Mousavi wins, you'll let me marry you . . ."

His future ex-wife bites her lip to contain her laughter and quickly winds up the window. A Mercedes pulls up, behind the wheel of which is a fly young man with spiked hair, a gold chain with a Zoroastrian pendant, and waxed eyebrows.

"What beautiful angels," the driver flatters them in his turn. "If only you were standing at the election, there would be no competition. You would both be president." The young man has hit the bull's-eye, much to Omid's disappointment. Numbers are scribbled onto a piece of paper, folded into quarters, and thrown from one window to another.

A little farther down, quite a different group of guests has arrived on the scene: a pack of around thirty members of the Basiji militia.

"*Chiz! Chiz! Chiz! Chiz!*" they chant over and over again, relishing the opportunity to mock Mousavi and his constant use of the word *chiz* (thing) throughout tonight's televised debate.

Far from intimidated, one young man opposite has already come up with a retort. "Rather *chiz* than *bi hameh chizeh*, [Rather 'thing' than 'nothing at all': a jibe at Ahmadinejad's plans]," which is quickly adopted by the entire crowd.

Another reveler holds up a packet of potato chips and begins to shout, "*Chitoz! Chitoz! Chitoz!*" in reference to the Iranian brand of chips of that name, whose mascot is a monkey.

The crowd bursts out laughing and begins to chant in unison, "Unless he cheats, Ahmadi will come in fifth," an amusing statement, given that there are only four candidates in the election.

Still farther down the street, amidst deafening whistles and green banners stretching up to twenty or thirty feet, a vehicle with an open trunk shows off a state-of-the-art, high-power subwoofer. Contrary to what one might expect, *damboulikossac* music—a popular Iranian genre, officially outlawed in the country and intended to inspire listeners to shake their behinds to the beat—blares from the car speakers. The party is in full flow. In the middle of the road, a young man works his way forward, his hips drawing circles in the air.

"*Eyval, eyval* [Bravo]," the crowd replies in time with the thumping bass.

The dancer is soon joined by a pretty young woman who launches into a sacred Eastern dance routine. Holding her head up proudly and pouting her lips in a bid to make herself even more desirable, she gradually begins to shake her entire body, starting at the shoulders and working her way down: arms, breasts, belly, and finally, her behind. This is a hard scene to believe in an Islamic Republic where women are forbidden to dance in public at all. Before long there are dozens of young men and women mingling together as they get down to the latest Iranian dance hit, egged on by the clapping accompaniment of the older members of the crowd who surround the scene. It is a display which would make even the Black Eyed Peas blush.

"We've been waiting for this for thirty years," sighs twenty-three-year-old Mahsa. "You know, there isn't much we can do around here to have fun."

A few women have even dared remove their headscarves and are using them as lassos to catch their male prey, a sign that soda may not have been the only thing on offer this evening. Several dancers don green glo-bracelets of the kind typical in Parisian nightclubs, while others carry green balloons, which they will later release into the sky.

"Have you ever seen such a huge club?" shouts Omid. "Even the Paris Techno Parade isn't this big."[1]

Amused and taken in by the crowd, even a few young policemen can be seen tapping their feet to the beat.

"Make the most of it, my friends," one of them laughs. "You who dare to say that Ahmadinejad denies you freedom."

"Shut the hell up," Omid mutters under his breath. "He's making fun of us, that guy, and right before the presidential election, too . . ."

In response, the young partiers play along, testing the officers' patience with their latest cry. "It's been a week, maybe two, since Mahmoud last took a bath."

No reaction; some officers are even caught with a smile on their faces. The butt of the joke here is the president's hair, which over the last four years has frequently appeared to be rather greasy and in need of a good shampoo. A couple of weeks ago and a comment such as that would have landed them in prison. On a roll, they step it up a level.

"A year ago, maybe two, Mahmoud ran out of clothes."

Still no reaction. This time, it's the head of state's worn-looking suit, the same one he has been wearing for four years, which falls victim to their mockery.

Omid cannot believe his eyes. "What's happened to the Islamic Republic?" he screams with joy. He sends a text message to everyone in his address book to ensure that not a single one of his friends misses out on this momentous occasion. Opposite Mellat Park (People's Park), a giant screen and set of speakers are being installed, on which young members of the Mir-Hossein Mousavi camp will show two campaign films.

"*Damesh garm*," cries Meysam, a twenty-four-year-old from South Tehran, who has never seen a spectacle like it. "Your president of the republic is one cool guy."

The avenue is at maximum capacity. The last people to arrive—families, women in chadors, grandparents, and the rich as well as the poor—join the scene, forming a green wave which stretches over twelve miles from the far north of the capital to the south.

"*Ey* Iran, *Ey* bejeweled land," sings the glorious crowd. These are the words of the country's unofficial national anthem, proudly sung by the Iranian people for the last sixty years, regardless of the regime. The older generation rejoices, and many of the Tehran inhabitants present tonight film the scene on their cell phones, immortalizing the moment and embracing a new way to share the event with the rest of the world.

A group of bikers in green bandanas, Bruce Lee–style, rips through the street as the riders slalom between the members of the crowd. Large numbers of them have come up from the more working-class southern areas of Tehran to get a taste of this exclusive party, the likes of which they have never before been invited to.

Overcome by emotion, one of them savors his moment of glory, shouting, "If you're here for Mousavi . . ."

". . . put your hands in the air!" is the crowd's response. One gets the distinct impression that there are not a great number of Ahmadinejad—or even Mehdi Karoubi—supporters at tonight's event.

The thirty or so Basijis and their famous chants of "*Chiz! Chiz! Chiz!*" make their appearance amidst the crowd's boos. There is nothing to fear, however, as the atmosphere remains playful. Omid and his friends talk back.

"When the creep can't think of anything else to say, he has a go at someone else's wife," a reference to the attack on Mousavi's wife during the debate. And they do not stop at that.

"Everyone felt the inflation, even Karoubi's own mother, everyone except that loser Ahmadi."

A car parked nearby turns up the volume on the stereo and blasts out a new *damboulikossac* tune, which gets the whole crowd going again. In time with the music, Omid dances just inches from the militiamen before starting a chant that will soon be taken up by the entire crowd. Furious, the Basiji remain stoic—a wise decision given that for the first time in their lives, they are in the minority. Suddenly the music stops. Next up, following on from the *damboulikossac*, is none other than French DJ David Guetta and his track "When Love Takes Over". The young partiers jump in every direction and parents, who have been testing out a few moves since earlier on, must finally admit defeat. Spotting a handful of foreign journalists who have arrived to cover the scene, their children suddenly take up a new refrain.

"*Ahmadi, bye-bye. Ahmadi, bye-bye,*" they shout, waving good-bye with their hands.

Valiasr Street was not the only host of festivities tonight. The party was in full swing in all four corners of the capital, including the south, which is often considered to be a more traditional section of the city. The Islamic Republic has seen large celebrations in the past, most memorably after its soccer team qualified for the World Cup in 1998, but such events have never lasted longer than one night.

"The authorities used them as safety valves," Omid recounts. "They allowed us one night to vent our frustrations and then reclaimed the upper hand."

This year, the celebrations will continue throughout the twenty nights of the campaign, welcoming new guests at every turn and offering them, for the first time in their lives, a taste of real freedom. The hope that these people have invested in Mousavi is immense, and it is hard to imagine that they will allow the Islamic Republic to reclaim their rights. Whatever the case, at four o'clock in the morning—with a few looking decidedly tipsy—the final slogan rings true.

"If there is fraud, Iran will explode. If there is fraud, Iran will explode."

6

As the sun rises over Valiasr Street, Tehran's hangover kicks in. The local share taxis have reclaimed their territory. Two boys are kicking around a striped plastic ball while a group of older men bets on pigeons; the man with the pigeon who stays in the air the longest will win the cash. We are at the Mowlavi intersection, in the south of the city. Twenty-four-year-old Reza steps out of the modest shack which he shares with his parents and five brothers and sisters, and sets off to work. He is a customer sales representative in a computer store downtown where he earns a salary of $415 per month, the average in Iran. In the afternoon, he leaves the store to take on his second role of the day: share taxi driver. He and a friend clubbed together to buy a Paykan, a 1960 Iranian-made rust pile for which they paid the modest sum of $5,700. The supplementary monthly income of $720 allows him to support his family. At ten o'clock at night, he stops in briefly at the shisha lounge before heading home where his mother has prepared him a delicious *ghormeh sabzi*.

In the last presidential election four years ago, Reza, like the rest of his family, voted for Ahmadinejad. Was this because he is an Islamist at heart, someone who wishes to see a return to the fundamental principles of the revolution? Far from it.

"Ahmadinejad promised that he would put oil money on our tables. And, quite honestly, he seemed like the lesser of two evils. The other option was former President Rafsandjani, the embodiment of corruption itself." Reza does not have anything good to say about Ahmadinejad's predecessor, the reformist Khatami, either.

"During his eight-year term as the country's head, all he concentrated on was shortening our women's skirts and taking care of the privileged kids in the north of the capital. He did absolutely nothing for the working classes." This time period saw the country's class divide rise to such unmanageable levels that the young man's entire neighborhood was lining up to vote for the ultraconservative candidate. Today, however, Reza is still kicking himself for it.

"The price of meat has doubled. Bread has risen to five times its previous amount, and that's before we even get to gas prices. Is that what they call social justice?" The end of the month is always hard for Reza and his family, and the retirement bonus which his father recently received will not stretch very far.

"Why has this only just been offered to us now, after four years of presidency?" the young man asks. This is one of the reasons for which Reza is ready, this time, to cast his vote for Mousavi and for change.

"He is the only one who can stand in the way of Ahmadinejad's reelection," he explains.

However, not all of his neighbors share his opinion, perhaps largely due to the infamous 50,000 tomans checks recently handed out in abundance. Add to this the fact that Mousavi's reformist plans are not in keeping with the issues which concern them most, and it is easy to understand why they plan, once again, to vote for the ultraconservative candidate.

"It will be a stupid mistake if they do," the young man sighs. "But unfortunately in Iran today, people think with their stomachs."

Freedom, women's rights, the repression going on within universities—these issues are of no great concern to Reza. But nor does he feel particularly strongly about the "morality police," whose presence around the capital has multiplied since Ahmadinejad's government took over four years ago.

"They've done a good job, returning order around here," he admits. "People were acting as if they were in a Hollywood movie, not the Islamic Republic." All the same, this young man who worships the eleven imams, sheds tears at their remembrance ceremonies, and always takes part in the Ramadan fast, still likes to permit himself a few small pleasures when night falls. It is not uncommon, for example, to see him buying a bottle of denatured alcohol with friends, to distill later at home with vanilla. And while his name may not figure on the guest lists of the wild parties going on around the capital, he can be found, one night a week, at the city airport—the only other place that's "happening" at night—with the hope of chatting up a few cute girls.

Despite his fairly modest income, the young man is (according to his own testimony) quite the heartbreaker, and claims to have several "gf's" (girlfriends). "Of course I do! What kind of a guy did you take me for? I have several *koss*, girls I sleep with on a regular basis."

Make no mistake, however, for as soon as he has enough money to "take a woman," as the saying goes, he too will allow his beloved mother to select a nice *najib* Iranian girl for him. On this same subject, Reza watches vigilantly over his sister in order to be sure that she has no "bf's" (boyfriends) of her own.

"It's a question of honor," he warns. Nevertheless, his sister spends many an afternoon hour alone in her room, chatting online.

The other topic which has taken center stage over the last four years is the nuclear program, described by the incumbent president as the "inalienable right of the Iranian people," a belief which has dragged the country into deep international crisis. On this subject, the young man quotes the official slogan: "Atomic energy, only thirty cents a case." which causes him to laugh out loud.

"Atomic energy is the least of our worries," he explains. "And anyway, didn't they announce on the television that we have it already?"

As for international politics, Reza, the fan of MTV's sexy music videos that he is, harbors no bad feelings towards the United States. His concerns lie elsewhere. "What I don't understand is why Palestine and Hezbollah get so much money while we in Iran are dying of hunger."

Reza was born in the Islamic Republic and therefore grew up surrounded by mullahs. While he may well curse them occasionally (do not tell anyone . . .), particularly in tough times, he quickly catches himself and begs forgiveness from above.

"People say that they can turn you into a cockroach," he whispers, deadly serious. Clearly, despite leaving the mosque many years ago, this young man is still very much a superstitious believer, and the

Islamic Republic knows exactly which buttons to press to get what it wants. The walls of the house are covered with portraits of Imam Ali, a figure worshipped by the Iranian people. His mother and sisters only leave the house in their chadors and spend their days confined to the kitchen or carrying out other household chores.

"That's just how we were raised," he says, defensively. All the same, Reza often falls victim to the violent temper of his mother, a woman who is never at a loss for words. There are, however, a good many things which are dealt with exclusively by his father, most importantly the family cash flow. "He's our very own supreme leader," the young man smiles.

Reza does not read the newspaper or any books and prefers to spend his time playing *futsal* (indoor soccer). As a result, the ferocious censorship of the press and publishing, enacted by Ahmadinejad since his election in 2005, has completely passed him by. Nor does he follow any blogs, which seems strange given that Iran ranks second only to Brazil in terms of the highest number of blogs published within one country. The only things that really get to him are the outrageously slow Internet speed, inconvenient filtering, and untimely connection problems, all of which interrupt his beloved Facebook and Yahoo! chat where he meets girls and enjoys raunchy photos (videos would take far too long to download).

Seven days away from the presidential election and our taxi driver does not seem particularly preoccupied by the campaign, or concerned about the green wave which is preparing to sweep across the country at this very moment. "It's just a few kids out to have a good time, that's all. Nothing serious."

Reza just hopes that the new president, whoever he may be, will think for once of those Iranians who go hungry. "You know, if it weren't for the corruption in the high ranks of the state, if we finally benefitted from the oil money, then this regime would be a paradise on earth."

7

*T*HE MELANCHOLIC OPENING arpeggios of Coldplay's "Clocks" fill the air followed by powerful guitar chords and the beginning of an energetic percussion accompaniment. From the middle of nowhere, an angelic yet piercing voice rings out.

"Lights go out and I can't be saved, tides that I tried to swim against."

We are in Niavaran, an affluent neighborhood of North Tehran, in a garage belonging to Kian, twenty-five-year-old singer and guitarist. At the keyboard is Sassan, also twenty-five and Kian's best friend, and on the drums we have Koushyar, twenty-six, a college friend. All three have matte complexions, long hair, and thick beards—what is referred to here as the "artist look."

Tonight this group of musicians will be performing Coldplay's greatest hits. Kian continues.

"Troubles that can't be named, tigers waiting to be tamed."

The artists are on cloud nine, as if on another planet, carried away by the music that they play so perfectly. As the song comes to an end, however, even the applause coming from the few friends who have gathered for the show cannot hold back the tears that betray their true distress. The three artists are completely demoralized.

"My garage," the singer laughs nervously. "This is what we have been reduced to: playing in a hovel like this." Kian takes a shot of *Aragh Sagi.*

The three friends have not always suffered in hiding. In the past, under the reformist President Khatami, the group released three albums, both in English and in Persian, and even received authorization to hold a number of public concerts in a park in the north of the city.

"It totally rocked. We'd sell a hundred tickets in a matter of hours. The crowds loved it."

Then, four years ago, came Ahmadinejad's victory and with it, the end of their career. "The Ministry of Culture and Islamic Guidance, which is now controlled by a bunch of ultraconservatives, immediately took away all of our authorizations. Our albums were taken off the shelves and we were forced underground."

Not only rock and metal groups but also a number of rap artists, such as Hichkas and Kiosk, have also risen up within this underground network, giving voice to their deep discontent.

While many young people are quick to criticize the reformist ex-president Khatami for his superficial offers of freedom, Kian jumps to his defense. "It was certainly no paradise, but at least we could play freely. When I was eighteen, I was a Metallica fan and could easily find their CDs on the black market. I'll never forget the day that I actually saw their official lyrics book in the store, on full display, translated into Persian. I couldn't believe my eyes, it was the happiest day of my life. And after that came Pink Floyd then Nirvana . . ." His cheerful expression quickly fades. "Then along came that scumbag and took them all off the shelves."

Thoroughly dejected, he returns to his guitar.

"*Sunlight, opened up my eyes, to see for the first time, you'll open them up.*"

This Coldplay track, "Twisted Logic," is much slower but allows for just as much expression as the others in the run-up to the chorus where the guitarist holds nothing back.

"*You'll go backwards, but then, you'll go forwards again . . . You'll go backwards, but then, you'll go . . .*" At the end of the song, Kian lights up a joint.

"This song is for my friends in prison—in prison because a select few have decided that our music is a symbol of Western decadence." He takes another shot of *Aragh* and continues angrily. "And anyway, even if you're lucky enough to slip through the net, there's no way you could ever make a living from your music. In Iran, you're doomed to failure before anyone has even had a chance to listen to you."

Kian comes from a fairly wealthy family and works as a sales representative in a sports equipment store, a job which provides him a little extra financial stability. Despite abandoning his psychology studies three years ago, he need not worry much about his future, and his father recently suggested that he take over the reins at the family textile factory. For the young man, however, this proposal is anything but attractive.

"I'm dying here. I just can't do this anymore. We're fed religion morning, noon, and night—at school, on TV. They've killed our country's culture. They decide what's good or bad for us, but the only thing they've managed to do is to turn us away from Islam."

The young man is quick to admit that he believes in "his own God" and even occasionally mentions the Shiite imams, for whom he holds a deep respect. Around his neck is a gold Farahvar pendant, a symbol of Zoroastrianism, the world's first monotheistic religion, which dates back to the Persian Empire more than three thousand years ago. Many young Iranians find, in the glory of this pre-Islamic period, a place in which to quell their immense frustration.

"We are Persian people, descendants of one of the oldest and most tolerant civilizations on earth," the singer likes to remind people. "It was the Arabs who invaded our country and, in so doing, have ruined it." He takes another hit as the tears roll down his cheek.

To forget their troubles, many of Kian's generation have turned in desperation to street drugs (hash, marijuana, speed, opium) or antidepressants. "The people that sell these pseudoremedies are the very ones who created the illness in the first place," he laughs again. The cure, however, is no longer enough. "The only thing that the Islamic Republic has done for us is that by submitting us to this daily torment, they have fueled our artistic creativity. Iran is a melting pot of talent, and on many different levels: research, science, music, film, visual arts . . . we have so much to express, so much to give . . . and they have reduced it all to nothing. The final insult is that now they are forcing us to leave the country we love so much."

Whatever the result of the upcoming presidential election, the young man has made up his mind. Just like his friends before him, who now find themselves scattered in all four corners of the globe, he too is determined to leave, whatever the cost.

"On September 19, Coldplay are playing at Wembley Stadium in London. Whatever happens, we'll be there."

The group plans to make a new home for themselves in Her Majesty's kingdom where, in their words, "artists are thought of differently." But are they not afraid of the fierce competition they may suffer at the hands of the huge number of British rock bands, at the head of which are their famous idols?

"No sacrifice is too big for the honor of playing in the open," he sighs. "We have an entire lifetime to catch up on."

Nevertheless, there is one major problem which stands in their way: the visa, which the British authorities hand out sparingly, an unfair response to Ahmadinejad's aggressive politics. Whereas Kian may have the resources to buy his way around this obstacle, the same cannot be said for his bandmates, who were not born with such luck.

"We'll find a way," the singer reassures us.

Before his departure, the young musician counts on doing his country one final favor by voting for Mousavi. "Four years ago, despite the concert authorizations we were given from Khatami, I just couldn't stand to live under that regime anymore, and I decided to boycott the election, not to vote." Today, the singer understands the error of this decision.

"We didn't think it could get any worse than it was under Khatami, but we were wrong. As for the Islamic Republic, it will bury us alive."

As far as Kian is concerned, "if you have to live a life ruled by mullahs, then it should at least be with the best of the lot"—in other words, the reformist Mir-Hossein Mousavi. The guitarist has certainly not forgotten that it was these very same reformists who issued their authorizations all those years ago. Today, according to Kian, they are the only ones who can control the current crisis which is paralyzing the country and revive Iran's culture. They alone can help change the way the people of this country think, and this is by far the greatest task ahead.

"A couple weeks ago, a neighbor called the cops on our hideout, denouncing our 'satanic' music, a term he no doubt used because of our long hair and beards. It wasn't the first time and, one wad of cash later, we were in the clear."

Kian puts down his guitar and announces, in all seriousness, "Until the people wake up to what is happening and join together in solidarity, we are condemned to live in this hell."

The young man dreams (secretly, of course) of a day when he, now famous in the United Kingdom, will return triumphantly to Tehran, several days after the revolution, to organize a huge free concert—a freedom concert—with one hundred and twenty thousand people packed into the open-air Azadi (Freedom) Stadium.

"I'll invite the biggest stars from around the world as well as from Iran, and the show will be played on huge screens in every town in the country." He has it all planned out. "This concert will go down in history, and it *will* happen in my lifetime, I promise you. It's what my people deserve."

8

DESPITE THE BEATING SUN, huge lines snake around the sides of the country's mosques on Friday, June 12, 2009. Thanks to the women in black chadors, the young students, the elderly men leaning on canes, and the clusters of hip, stylish girls in attendance, there is a wait of at least two hours to get inside. Could it be that the Islamic Republic has finally gotten what it wanted, that Islam has come back into fashion?

"Long live Imam Hossein. Long live Mir-Hossein Mousavi," chant the hundred or so delighted Iranians in the long line. As you have probably guessed, today is Election Day in Iran.

A few worrying signs are already beginning to emerge. All text messaging, the principal weapon in the Mousavi camp, is down; the network is simply not working. Those gathered, however, do not seem too concerned at this stage of the game.

"Unless he cheats, Ahmadinejad will come in fifth," they shout in one voice, a smile on every face.

Among the crowd is a young woman whose bangs and long brown hair hang loose from her headscarf. Her coat is formfitting, her makeup pronounced, and her Christian Dior sunglasses add the final touch of what the Iranian people call *kelass* (style). This beautiful woman's name is Azadeh and she is twenty-five years old. As for the chants, she seems to be having trouble keeping up, but this should not be held against her. Today will be the first time she has ever voted and, understandably, she is feeling more than a little emotional. Four years ago, she was among those who decided to boycott the election.

"Voting for the president just shows that you support this discrim-inatory regime and their 'election,' where every candidate has been hand-picked by the system," she explains.

So what brings her out here today, in this unbearable heat? "I'm here today to put a stop to you-know-who [Ahmadinejad], even if it means voting for another 'son of the regime.'" This is how she chooses to describe her number one choice, the reformist Mousavi.

The majority of people in line today are wearing green ribbons and/or headscarves, symbols of the movement established by the 'son of the regime' to whom she refers. Could it be that, seven months after Barack Obama's election to the White House, this land of the mullahs is witnessing a similar "Mousavimania"?

"Not at all," the young woman replies dryly. "Mousavi is the best . . . of the worst, simple as that."

At this very moment, a green supporter, his ear pressed up against the radio on his cell phone, announces that a member of the Revolutionary Guard, the regime's ideological army, has just issued a warning that he will not "tolerate any kind of green velvet revolution."

"*Baba* [Ha-ha]," the man whoops with joy. "It sounds like they're taking us seriously." He bursts out laughing.

"What happened to the crows?" a young man suddenly cries from afar.

"Flown away forever," the young woman joins the crowd of voters as they respond in chorus, laughter coming from all around. These lyrics are from a children's nursery rhyme, whose words are now adapted to the amusement of all.

"And the sparrows?" the young man continues.

"Flown away forever," the crowd chants.

"What happened to the lies?" he goes one better.

"Flown away forever,"

"And Mahmoud?" he finally asks.

"Flown away forever!" they now sing in unison before bursting into a round of unanimous applause. According to those present today, this kind of atmosphere has not been felt since the reformist Mohammad Khatami was elected twelve years ago, an occasion which saw over 70 percent of Iranians, new voters for the most part, travel en masse to vote for Khatami and for change. Disappointment soon spread, however, and became a major factor in the mass abstention and consequential victory of the ultraconservative Ahmadinejad eight years later, in 2005.

"But today," Azadeh is proud to announce, "the younger generation is back with a vengeance."

As well as the country's youngsters, many women, intellectuals, their families, and pretty much everybody who boycotted the election four years ago have now come out in force to block the incumbent president's reelection.

"*May* I?" the young man from earlier starts up again.

"Be my guest . . ." the crowd cries.

"*May* I?" he repeats.

"Be my guest . . ."

What they refer to here, of course, is Ahmadinejad's underhand questioning of Mousavi's wife during the televised debate. This particular exchange, which quickly became a big hit, is now a favorite joke in Iranian households looking to make fun of the ultraconservative.

Swept up in the emotion of the moment, Azadeh allows her excitement to show. "Victory is in the bag. Look around, everyone here is in green."

"*Eyval* [Bravo]," the crowd yells.

At twenty-five, Azadeh is a perfect example of the modern Iranian woman. But woe betide anyone who calls her Azadeh, or even Azi (her nickname), to her face. A recent graduate in mechanical engineering from the prestigious University of Tehran, she prefers to be known as *khanoom doctor* (literally, Madam Doctor).

"Iranian women are making amazing progress," she states. "How many people can claim to truly know how to reconcile professional life with traditional domestic life as we do?"

Azadeh—I mean, *khanoom doctor*—is not wrong. Today, women make up over 65 percent of the student population in Iranian universities. They often climb to positions of responsibility (members of parliament, CEOs, pilots) and have had the right to vote since 1963, a far cry from Iraq, Afghanistan, or Saudi Arabia, where women are not permitted to drive, let alone to vote. Iran's 2009 presidential campaign turned a corner in political history as candidates' wives, for the first time in thirty years, played a leading role alongside their husbands. One example was Mousavi's wife, the highly qualified Zahra Rahnavard or, as Azadeh corrects, "Doctor Rahnavard."

The sixty-five-year-old former director of Al-Zahra University in Tehran, who was relieved of her professional duties by Mahmoud Ahmadinejad, is a doctor of political science and also holds a master of arts. She barely left her husband's side during the electoral campaign; such dedication has led many to refer to her as the Iranian "Michelle Obama." Often dressed in a flowery chador, she has never been afraid of speaking publicly and denouncing the Islamic Republic's "discriminatory laws against women." For while it may be true that women are in the majority at universities, there are still many unfair laws as far as their other interests are concerned. The age of majority for women remains at nine years old (as opposed to sixteen for men), and their testimony in court is technically worth half that of an Iranian man. Girls are only entitled to half as much inheritance as their brothers, and within a couple, guardianship of any children is given solely to the father. If the father should die without giving prior consent to his wife, then it is the paternal grandfather or a court of law who takes over as guardian. Perhaps the worst of all is the "blood-price" issue whereby the money owed to a murder victim's family by the guilty party is divided by two if that victim is a woman.

This all goes a long way in explaining why Azadeh has come out to take her place in this long line this morning. Since 2006, she has also been a member of the international campaign *One Million Signatures*, which won the Simone de Beauvoir Prize in 2009. This project is dependent on the hard work of young activists like Azadeh, who go door to door collecting signatures, as well as on celebrities such as Iranian lawyer Shirin Ebadi. Their collective goal is to obtain one million signatures from around the country and overseas to the end of changing Iranian legislation. Through this relentless campaigning, they have already had some success in repealing a number of Ahmadinejad's laws.

"In September 2008," *khanoom doctor* explains, "Ahmadinejad wrote what he called the 'Family Protection Bill,' which he wanted to pass through parliament. Article 23 of the act stated that a man could practice polygamy without prior consent from his first wife as long as he obtained a simple permit from the government. Article 25 stated that any *mehrieh* [dowry] owed by a husband to his wife at the time of divorce would be subject to taxation." She loses her temper. "Can you imagine? Taxing the one benefit that a woman gets from marriage?" Thanks to persistent pressure from feminists of the same caliber as Azadeh, these two articles were finally removed from the bill.

Aside from this law, another of the ultraconservative government's programs has particularly affected the daily lives of Iranian women over the last few years: the increased presence of the "morality police." As a direct consequence of this, many women have been roughed up and abused in the street by these government agents for the simple reason that their outfits were deemed to be too Western. Azadeh has had first-hand experience of this, and the memories are not pleasant.

"A group of 'Ahmadinejad girls' just grabbed a hold of me in the street, talking down to me as if I were a prostitute, all because the pants I was wearing were too short. I cried and cried, but they just didn't care. They threw me in a truck and took me to the station where I had to sign a statement promising never to cause a public security risk like that again. They're just a bunch of frustrated old crones, and with their stupid moustaches too . . ." Luckily, she can laugh about it now.

Despite such occurrences, and the fact that the Islamic Republic currently enforces the veil more than ever before in its history, the young woman is fairly calm about the situation. "Of course I would rather not wear it," she explains, "but unlike our mothers, we grew up wearing the veil. These days, the problem lies elsewhere."

For this reason, the One Million Signatures campaign, as well as its goal of achieving legal reform, concentrates on changing mentalities, particularly in less-developed villages, by promoting dialogue with both men and women in order to encourage egalitarian discussion.

"Unfortunately," Azadeh sighs, "there are still many, many women out there who don't even know that they have rights and many men who are macho and sexist."

It is not unusual for this charming and elegant young woman to be harassed in the street, sometimes even to have her backside pinched, simply because she dares to walk alone in high heels. "I'm the first to admit that the mullahs are hugely responsible for creating this perverted environment," she says. "But it's also the responsibility of these individual men to educate themselves and to broaden their minds, and they still have a long way to go."

Fighting for this cause could easily lead to time in prison. "I'll never forget the day in June 2006 when we were attacked by the security forces, just for conducting a peaceful demonstration, for protesting for our rights." A look of horror crosses her face as she remembers.

Since 2006, around one hundred members of the collective claim to have been beaten, arrested, or put on trial for collecting signatures in public spaces, and some have even been forced to flee the country. According to Iran's government, they were guilty of "acting against national security and distributing propaganda against those currently in power."

"It's the same old accusation they use every time someone annoys the Islamic Republic," Azadeh sighs with a hint of malice, for none of this is enough to dissuade our young friend. "If that's the price we have to pay for change, then I'll pay it."

As far as she is concerned, Iran's future includes women whether the ayatollahs like it or not. "It is only thanks to the courage and determination of women that today, thirty years on from the advent of the Islamic Revolution, we're not all locked away at home in our chadors. That we are active members of society."

So will the Iranian women's movement join forces with the Green Movement? "First and foremost, I'm a feminist"—she smiles—"but today, our priority is to elect Mousavi."

All of a sudden, Azadeh is gone, disappearing inside the mosque. It is hard to describe the level of excitement which reigns in the room she now enters, despite the slightly disconcerting Basiji presence around the ballot boxes.

"It's just impossible. There is no way that they can suppress this kind of enthusiasm." She seems convinced. She approaches the official, a bearded, smiling man; hands over her passport, as yet devoid of any stamp; and dips her finger in the purple ink. She takes the single voting slip, which carries the names of the four candidates, before marking her choice. On exiting the building, she proudly raises her stained index finger to the crowd, who answer her with their cheers.

"*Damesh garm. Damesh garm* [Bravo]."

Azadeh cannot hold back the tear which rolls down her cheek. "Oh, how I love my people."

No sooner has she left the mosque, however, than rumors begin to circulate about a shortage of voting skips at several locations. "Don't worry"—Azadeh tries to put things in perspective—"they've always cheated in the past, but there's no way that they can destroy thirty million votes this time."

A second report: reformist officials have been prevented from properly monitoring vote counting in several areas. The hours tick by and more rumors emerge. Many voters are complaining that their polling stations closed early despite the crowds waiting outside.

At home, Azadeh is glued to BBC Persian where a discussion is in full swing about reported ballot-stuffing in mobile ballot boxes in the provinces. At the same time, state television is declaring, loud and clear, that the unprecedented participation means victory for the Islamic Revolution. Azadeh cannot stop herself from biting what is left of her fingernails. In just a few minutes, the ordeal will be over.

9

*A*FTER A HUNDRED DAYS and a hundred and one nights of working around the clock, Arya is finally satisfied that the job has been done. "We, along with the thousands of young people who have worked alongside us, have done everything in our power, and then some, to ensure that Mousavi's message reaches every corner of Iranian society. And this time we have succeeded: victory will be ours."

The journalist might sound a little presumptuous, but he is basing his assumptions on reports from his teams around the country. "Our contacts, their friends, their families, and even the mosque muezzins: everybody promised to go out today and vote for Mousavi. This is going to be one hell of a celebration. We have all been waiting for this for so long."

At eight o'clock in the morning, the Ministry of Interior declares that the election campaign is officially over, meaning that no further canvassing or any other form of publicity will be allowed.

"The ball is in the voters' court now," Arya explains, "but the observers will also play a huge role as they rush to the four corners of the country to ensure that voting is carried out fairly."

When Ahmadinejad was elected for the first time four years ago, these same observers spoke of substantial irregularities, but threats from the supreme leader, and in particular from the Basij, succeeded in driving them into silence.

"*Inshallah*, that will not be the case this year," says Arya.

This, however, is by no means a sign that the young man has renewed his faith in the authorities. "It's just that pulling off the degree of fraud that it would take with such a huge turnout simply can't be possible."

Nevertheless, the journalist finds himself taking comfort in prayer. Today, he will be able to enjoy his first day off in a long, long time, and he has accepted an invitation which will take him to a large mountain villa, an hour outside of the capital, where a childhood friend is getting married. The ceremony will be a religious one, presided over by a mullah, but a huge party will follow, at which no dress shirts or shoes—or in this case no headscarves or manteaux—will be required;[1] a party at which Arya plans to show that just because you are politically active in Iran, it does not go without saying that you cannot hold your own on the dance floor. He would undoubtedly have won the votes of the entire room if it were not for the fact that, to the great disappointment of his fans, the young man is dead on his feet after just three *ghers* (a hip-swinging dance move).

The following day, after a much-deserved lie-in, Arya is back in the capital at his campaign headquarters. He is already losing patience with his cell phone: The text messages, upon which he constantly relies to send group information to his contacts, are not going through. His first thought is that there is a simple network problem, but as he switches on his laptop, it quickly becomes clear that the cause is something different altogether. The vast majority of reformist websites are also out of order. But no need to panic too much, as by noon the first bits of good news begin to trickle in from Isfahan, Tabriz, and Yazd.

"There are huge lines outside the polling stations. And they are all green," he learns.

"*Ya Ali*,"[2] the journalist shouts out, slamming his fist down on the table.

"What is it? Tell us," his young colleagues press him in excitement.

"It's a good start," Arya tells them before warning, "but remember, you must never offer the sacrificial doe if you have not already hunted her down."

Rumors continue to circulate; apparently, the pens given to voters contain erasable ink. No worries there as many people made it a point of honor to bring their own pens. As the day goes on, Arya's cell phone will not stop buzzing as more and more evidence confirms what they hoped would be true. It is no longer just the observers on the other end of the line but also a number of senior reformist figures.

"There's no longer any doubt, the gap is simply too great." Arya can shout it from the rooftops: "Mousavi's going to do it . . ."

Brimming with excitement, but nonetheless acting with restraint (as dictated by the Islamic Republic), Arya jumps in the car and heads off in the direction of Mir-Hossein Mousavi's campaign headquarters in the northern district of Gheytarieh. It is six o'clock in the evening, and he is surprised to find that the mood with the reformist candidate's right-hand men is far from celebratory. The atmosphere, in fact, is decidedly tense and apprehensive.

"The authorities have just announced that many polling stations didn't have enough ballot slips. As a result, they had to close," one of the movement's key figures fills him in.

"That's impossible," Arya cries. "It was seen to that the Ministry of Interior printed more than could possibly be needed by the number of voters."

There are more surprises to come.

"A number of polling stations are closing even though there are hoards of people trying to get in to cast their vote," he now learns. "In Yazd, the Friday Imam himself had to reopen the ballot boxes."

"*Khodaya.* What does all this mean?" Arya shouts. "They wouldn't dare . . . it's impossible."

His phone rings again with the news that antiriot police have blocked off the main entrances to the capital and are surrounding the Ministry of Interior. "This smells fishy to me. This many suspicious moves before the voting is even over . . . I have never seen this before."

Further rumors are beginning to circulate with such frequency that they can no longer be dismissed. "The police have been ordered to attack the campaign headquarters," someone warns him.

"Quick," Arya leaps into action. "Wipe your hard drives . . . hurry!"

The young men get to work while in front of the building a large crowd of security forces is gathering, accompanied by jubilant Ahmadinejad supporters.

"*Agha mohandes* [the boss] is going to talk," the journalist is told.

Arya rushes once more to his car to get to the district of Jordan where Mir-Hossein Mousavi is holding a press conference. "The room was packed," he remembers. "There were over two hundred journalists inside and another two hundred out front."

The scene is one of chaos, with one journalist screaming at the others to quiet down. Finally, the reformist candidate begins to speak.

"I am grateful to the people for their diligent participation in this election. Their presence was extraordinary, they were full of joy and cheer . . . Today we saw people going to the polling stations for the first time in their lives. The entire population bore witness to this, and we all feel its effects. An attendance as great as this has not been seen since the beginning of the revolution. The lines were so long in some places that many of you waited for as long as three hours to put your voting slips into the ballot box. The people believed that their participation in this election would lead to positive change in this country, and this is the proof of great motivation and of hope . . . I thank the dear people of this country for their joy, their cheer, and their sacrifice . . . However, and I will come back to this, the question now is whether the government has acted appropriately in light of today's events. I believe that it has not, that it does not recognize the value of what has taken place. According to information gathered from our campaign offices around the country, I have earned the highest number of votes and am therefore the definitive winner. This means that the people have voted for me.

"The final results will be issued in the near future . . . although around the country large numbers of our observers were sent away, our offices were attacked, and there were a great deal of problems with the delivery of voting slips. In many centers, where we know that huge numbers of voting slips were printed, people were apparently informed that there were none. This was the case in Tabriz, Isfahan, Shiraz, and in many other towns. We have seen that many polling stations were told to close as soon as possible, despite the fact that state television announced that voting hours were to be extended. Many people found themselves in front of barred doorways, and there they remain, unable to vote. We had been promised that if need be, hours would be extended, and that every person would be able to place their vote into a ballot box. It is outrageous that this promise has not been kept . . .

"The people have, nonetheless, accepted all of this, and we have information which shows that across the entire country, the participation in this election was immense and unprecedented. For this reason, dear journalists, I wish to tell you today that we recognize these things as mistakes, and that I—personally and with the support of the people—will follow up on them and will stop at nothing. We have started out on this path and we will not go back . . . I am convinced that the people's conscience, their knowledge, and their experience today will be the most reliable testimonies as to whether the government acted in honesty or not. In any case, and in accordance with the information we have received, we consider ourselves to be the winners of this election. We expect the count to happen in a manner that is precise, and that a reassuring response concerning these errors will be given to the people . . .

"We must respect the wishes of our citizens. Their choice and freedom were the principal goals of our sacred revolution. This is all we have ever hoped for, and I know that our dear people want for nothing more . . . We hope that the legal bodies concerned will apply the necessary measures, and we are confident that with the intelligence and experience of our supreme leader, this problem, *inshallah*, will be resolved."

Applause and cheering from all around; standing in the wings, Arya cries tears of joy. "What a speaker. What honesty. How could anyone not be moved by such a speech?" He is beside himself with joy, beaming with pride for his people. "We won. As Iranians, we have taken a giant leap towards democracy."

But there are also tears of pain, for Arya is well and truly wiped out. "You have to read between the lines. If *Agha mohandes* he is announcing his victory and at the same time hinting at the idea of large-scale fraud, this can only be meant as a prediction of something ominous."

The cheering in the room has subsided, and in its wake, a deathly silence looms.

"Everyone here gets it," Arya continues, exhausted. "But there is good news, and you heard it for yourselves: *Agha mohandes* will fight until the bitter end."

This prediction will prove to be correct. The axe falls just a few minutes later, at 11:00 p.m. in the form of a dispatch. The governmental agencies Raja News and Fars News are announcing the victory of Mahmoud Ahmadinejad, with 63 percent of the vote, before the count has even been completed. This result will be his final, official score.

"It's not Fars News, it's False News," Arya screams before bursting into tears. "It's a coup d'état . . ."

Back at headquarters, his colleagues agree unanimously and denounce the events as a coup. The Basijis, who have now been stationed outside the building for several hours, suddenly launch their attack.

"It was a full-blown raid," Arya remembers. "They ransacked *everything*. Dozens of my friends were arrested." Fortunately, the journalist manages to escape with a broken finger, but if there is one thing he is sure of, it is that he will not be sleeping at home tonight. And wherever he is, he will not sleep for long. The next day, his parents order him to leave the country.

"No way, I will not be seen as a coward. We didn't do all of this for nothing," he refuses.

A few hours later, he will meet the defeated candidate in person and whisper, "If you back down from this, we will never forgive you."

Throughout the West, there is utter amazement. While many media sources begin to uncover the extent of the fraud, many analysts do an about-turn and announce that they must simply have underestimated the popular support for Mahmoud Ahmadinejad.

"I'd like to believe that," Arya sniggers. "But if that were the case, then why bother with the raids?"

10

*T*HE SUN IS SETTING OVER the University of Tehran on Sunday, June 14, 2009. Still reeling from the shock of the previous day's events, Arya and his classmates from the most prestigious university in the country gather in a dorm room to discuss how to proceed. They have already received the news. Yesterday and this morning, around ten of the most prominent reformists behind Mir-Hossein Mousavi's campaign were arrested in their homes and taken to the infamous Evin Prison, accused of organizing mass demonstrations in the Iranian capital. Several held high positions in the government of former reformist President Khatami, and they include Behzad Nabavi, former deputy speaker of the Parliament; Mohsen Mirdamadi, head of the parliamentary foreign policy commission as well as one of the organizers of the hostage crisis at the American embassy in 1979; and Abdollah Ramezanzadeh, spokesperson for the Khatami government.

"This is insane," Arya cries. "The regime is locking up its *own* sons, the ones who led its revolution. They're trying to cut all ties between the reformist leaders and the population. This doesn't bode well . . . not well at all."

The young man and his fellow students, who all played major roles in the Mousavi campaign, have just a few months for the most part—a few years at most—to put up with life in the Islamic Republic before obtaining their degrees and, by extension, tickets to a bright future overseas.

"We can't just sit back and take this," he exclaims. "This time they've gone too far. They had everything set up perfectly, ready to do whatever it took to prevent us from having a choice. Despite everything we did, they found a way to cheat."

"But what exactly do you want to do about it?" replies Shahryar, his twenty-seven-year-old friend, a gifted student in the doctoral physics program. "You know as well as anyone that they're capable of getting rid of us, of picking us off, one by one . . ."

Almost exactly ten years ago, following the closure of the reformist daily newspaper *Salam*, demonstrations erupted in the dormitories at the University of Tehran. They were violently stamped out in the middle of the night by the Basij, and the following day, thousands of students descended into the streets of Tehran, then in other towns around the country. There was to be a huge price to pay for these actions: Seventeen people lost their lives, and over two hundred were injured.

"We have to do something," Arya continues, "whatever the cost, we can't let them insult us like this."

As the clock strikes 11:30 p.m., the two friends are awoken by screaming.

"They're trying to get in. Get up, move! They're trying to get into the dormitory . . ."

One glance out of the window is enough to understand the impending danger. Special police forces surround the university. On this point, however, Iranian law is clear: Security forces are strictly forbidden from entering Tehran's university residences.

"Don't panic," Khosrow, another student, tries to calm the situation. "They're just trying to intimidate us. They wouldn't dare enter."

Unfortunately, the young man is wrong. The officers, dressed in a black Robocop-style getup that would make even our riot police blush, have already made it through the first entrance grate and are setting things on fire. They are soon joined by plainclothes Basijis.

"Assholes. Destroying our votes wasn't enough for them? Now it's our turn?" Arya shouts.

"Everyone, up top," Khosrow orders. "They've stolen our country already, but they won't take our university."

"Corrupt government. Resign. Resign," the three friends and their peers now chant from the roof of their residence. The police reply by firing tear gas in their direction.

"Wrap a T-shirt or something around your nose," Khosrow shouts again as the students respond by throwing stones. A crowd has gathered opposite the university, helpless witnesses to the attack.

"Come on, help us," cries Arya. This is guerrilla warfare, pure and simple.

More halls are set alight by the *gardeh vijeh*, as the special police forces are known, and stones fly through the night skies from both sides.

"The orders to attack must have come from Rajabzadeh [Tehran's new police chief]," Shahryar is convinced.

Despite the fierce attack, the students hold their own, at least for now, thanks to their knowledge of the university campus, whose corridors they know like the backs of their hands.

"Basijis, call for reinforcements," comes the sudden cry from a large bearded man, his white shirt tucked into his pants. All the while, thick black smoke pours from the dormitories. One hour later, at about 2:30 a.m., assailants armed with Molotov cocktails and billy clubs finally break through the barriers at the entrance gate. Like wild animals, they charge towards the dormitories.

"Run!" Arya cries. "They'll kill us all."

The three friends hide together, *in extremis*, in the bathrooms of one of the residences. Many of their classmates will not be so lucky.

Horrific cries rise up into the Tehran night skies as the police finally penetrate the dormitories. Minutes later, their inhabitants are dragged out along the ground, beaten and defeated. In his hideout, Arya, out of breath from running and paralyzed with fear, bursts into tears.

"What scum—to think that it's our own countrymen who are killing us. Whether they're doing it for Ahmadinejad or for someone else, I don't care . . . how did we arrive at this point?"

Outside, four militiamen are kicking a lone young student, ordering him to get to his feet.

"Please, brothers, don't hit me. I beg you . . . Don't hit me . . ." he pleads. Shocked at such levels of gratuitous violence, one of their colleagues urges them to stop the massacre.

The residence library is the next target for the police attack; its occupants are dragged to the floor, savagely beaten and verbally insulted.

"Take his photo and kill him," one of the policemen cries as he points out one young man, barely more than a boy, curled up on the floor. Half a dozen bodies lie piled around him, like helpless animals. The surrounding Robocops take a dark pleasure in continuing to beat them.

"Suckers, you thought you could attack us?" one of them scoffs. The violence is so extreme that in the end, it is the Basiji officers themselves who beg the police to stop the carnage.

"Don't beat them. Leave them now, they've had enough. For Imam Hossein's sake . . ."

A stream of blood pours from one of the student's skulls while the others try as best as they can to protect their heads from the violent kicks. Suddenly, one of the assailants drops down to their level.

"Put your hands down, now. I'm talking to you . . . raise your head and look at me, come on!" The man captures their battered faces with his camera to help with later identification.

The following morning, the police have gone, leaving the building in ruins. There is no sign of any bodies; just a few pools of blood serve as a reminder of the horror of the previous day.

"It's hard to imagine that we used to actually study here," Arya, finally out of the bathroom, is sobbing. The dormitory doors are covered with axe marks. The computers have been smashed up, books have been burned. Worse still, several windows are still open, and below the fourth floor the bushes have obviously been disturbed.

"*Khodaya* [Oh my God]," Khosrow exclaims. "They threw them out of the window. They threw them out, just like they did ten years ago."

The three friends hold each other tight and burst into tears. This evening's events left so much destruction in their wake that the university residence will close its doors the following day, and all end-of-year exams will be cancelled. The student organization Tahkim Vahdat will announce the deaths of five students during the horrific incident, a number which will later be confirmed by *The Guardian*. Their names were Fatemeh Barati and Mobina Ehterami (two women), Kasra Sharafi, Kambiz Shoaee, and Mohsen Imani. The assumption is that they were buried the following day in a Tehran cemetery, without their families even being informed. The British newspaper will also report that forty-six students were taken that night to the fourth basement level of the building that houses the Ministry of Interior. The Iranian government will deny these figures, quoting between one hundred and one hundred twenty injuries. Supreme Leader Ayatollah Khamenei and President Mahmoud Ahmadinejad will put the blame, as always, on the "enemies" of the Islamic Republic: in other words, the West.

.

11

"*W*HERE'S MY VOTE? Where's my vote?"

The date is Monday, June 15, 2009, and Omid—he who claimed he had lost faith in everything—has decided to take to the streets for the first time in his life. The young man looks around, worried and unsure of what to expect. He can rest assured today though, safe in the knowledge that at least he is not alone. Like a human tidal wave, an estimated three million people are demonstrating at his side. Looking around, there is an awful lot of lace to be seen in the crowd and, of course, a great number of chadors. Omid, however, finds himself surrounded by an eclectic group including mothers covered from head to toe, fashionistas in loose headscarves, students, grandparents, and even a few injured war veterans. He is quite simply overwhelmed by the scene.

"*Dameshoon garm.* So where are the 63 percent that voted for Ahmadinejad?"

"Mousavi. Mousavi. We're here for you," the cries ring out. The crowd tries out what they call *shoar*, impromptu political slogans, often rhyming, which serve as a demonstration of Iranian inventiveness and sense of humor.

"Liar. Liar. Where is your 63 percent?" they now chant.

Some demonstrators don masks reminiscent of those worn in the Gaza Strip to avoid being recognized. The march will cover over four and a half miles, setting off from the crossroads at Enghelab (Revolution) Square and ending at Azadi (Freedom) Square, retracing the exact route taken thirty years ago during the 1979 revolution. Outside the capital, demonstrations have erupted in other main cities around the country, including in Shiraz, in the holy city of Mashad, and in Isfahan.

The two former reformist candidates Mir-Hossein Mousavi and Mehdi Karoubi have now joined forces, and it is they who originally called their supporters to the streets today. They were forced, however, to retract that call after the Ministry of Interior refused to issue an authorization for the march. In Iran, to demonstrate without authorization is to risk your life, but even this will not stop anyone today, and hundreds of thousands of Iranians opt to take the risk by spontaneously joining together in the streets. This does not mean that they are not afraid, and there is good reason to be so: mobile phone service has been suspended and Internet connections considerably slowed down. Foreign journalists have been asked to remain in their hotels. No one can quite shake the memory of the violent repression of student demonstrations a decade ago, which saw many protesters slaughtered in the middle of the street and led to the disappearance of a great number of others.

"But just look around," Omid points out today. "This isn't just students; an entire population has come out to the street today. *Mashallah mardomeh Iran* [Bravo to the Iranian people]."

"Iranians choose death over humiliation," the crowd scolds. Nobody can deny that they have been humiliated, and just the day before their "reelected president," Mahmoud Ahmadinejad, referred to them as nothing but "dirt and dust," adding with an accidental hint of irony that Iran's elections were the "cleanest" in the world.

"Dust?" shouts Reyhaneh, a young woman dressed from head to toe in green. "We'll give him a dust storm if that's what he wants."

Despite the atmosphere of excitement, Omid is still in disbelief. "Why did he have to cheat on this scale?" he cannot stop asking himself. "How could they underestimate us to this extent? They could just as easily have had him win by a small margin, in the second round, and that would have been that . . . ." Could this possibly be the start of another revolution?

"*Na Baba* [Not at all]," he replies firmly. "Let's just wait and see what happens. I don't know what's going to come of it, but the Iranian people are furious. They have been betrayed in the worst possible way, and today they are in the streets to reclaim their vote."

"Mousavi. Mousavi. Give us back our vote." This new cry comes from a student who admits that he himself did not even vote.

"Death to the dictator, be it a shah or doctor." This slogan comes from a nearby woman, a mother in a black chador. The chant is quickly picked up by tens and then hundreds of protesters. This is a big deal; the word is finally out there. For the first time in thirty years, a head of the Islamic Republic is being called a dictator.

"*Mashallah*," Omid smiles. "Iranians will never cease to amaze me. It's clever: by leaving out Ahmadinejad's name and referring to him simply by his title of 'doctor,' they will avoid brutal repercussions."

Among the crowd, an elegant woman, visibly emotional, holds up a V for victory finger sign. She is still wearing her large Christian Dior sunglasses, but this time it is to avoid identification.

"Of course I'm afraid, but I'm so happy," Azadeh manages to get out in between laughter and tears. "Just look around you, there are as many women out here as men. The atmosphere is amazing. The Iranian people made this happen, they have dared to say no to fear. Bullets, tanks, cannons: none of that will stop us now," the young woman cries at the top of her lungs.

Completely overwhelmed, the police follow the march with their eyes. "Join us, brothers. You should be on our side," Azadeh insists, holding out a rose as a sign of peace.

"*Khanoom* [Miss]"—the police officer grins—"why don't you give me your phone number?"

"*Aïe kessafat* [Sleazebag]," she laughs in his face. To her right, a similarly elegant woman claps her hands, a few gray strands escaping her green headscarf. This is Mandana, Azadeh's mother. For years she has begged her daughter to stop risking her life in the streets, but this morning, it was she who woke the girl up to join her.

"I haven't seen this many people since *our* revolution," she sobs behind her glasses.

"Shhhh." Each protester turns to his or her neighbor, whispering in an Iranian version of the game "telephone."

"The authorities have forbidden us to demonstrate," Azadeh explains quietly. "We must do as they say." The young woman takes her mother's hand, as well as that of the person to her left, an elderly man of around seventy, and lifts them up toward the sky. They march forward, hand in hand, without saying a word. This sight must be a first: millions of Iranians, of all classes and generations, marching in churchlike silence.

"It's the only way not to get killed," whispers an amputee on crutches as he passes before the dumbfounded police officers.

Stunned, Azadeh sheds another tear. "I was wrong. I never believed that Iranians could display quite this much solidarity."

The only things visible above this human wave are the V for victory finger signs, a few cell phones, green ribbons, and placards. On the latter, the statements *Ahmadinejad is not my president* and *Where is my vote*, clearly written in English, are directed at the foreign press. Accused by supreme leader Ayatollah Khamenei, of waging a "psychological war against Iran," foreign journalists have been forbidden from attending the march. The few that managed to escape their "guardian angels" at the hotel are pounced upon by the protesters.

"Now you can see that Iranian people are different from their government," a young Iranian woman shouts in English, with a thick Farsi accent. "Tell your people we want freedom."

The young—and quite beautiful—woman takes the journalist by the arm and leads him through the crowd to her house without a second thought as to what her parents may think. Once they reach her bedroom, she pushes him towards a chair . . . setting him up in front of her computer so that he may send off his report without further delay. Unfortunately, testing out the Internet speed, which is running catastrophically slowly, the journalist quickly realizes that it is a lost cause. Still, there is no need to panic too much; they may have managed somehow to dispose of all video cameras, but the time has come to welcome the cell phone, millions of which will film every last detail, in the darkest of alleyways, their owners rushing straight to the Internet to upload their content to Twitter, YouTube, and Facebook. Filters may well have been put in place as damage control, with networks slowed down or even cut; but fortunately, the Iranian people are masters at the art of resourcefulness.

Seated at a desk at an office supply company site, Arya is busy uploading the latest videos, passed along to him by his Mousavi camp comrades, to YouTube. The journalist would much rather be among the crowd, alongside his fellow people, on this historic day. "But what's the point if no one ever finds out about it?" he asks.

It was Hamid, company director and older brother of a friend of Arya's cousin, who opened his door to the young man. "We are all Iranians," he explains proudly. "It's time to stand together against these people."

The company is lucky enough to have an Internet connection speed of 512K, four times that offered to individuals who Ahmadinejad decided could be made to make do with the limited 128K. Arya and a dozen other "green-thumbed" youngsters have been working around the clock since Saturday to send out content, not just from their own cell phones, but also from those of their friends and cousins whose phones have been rendered useless by the network cuts.

"Good thing it's not 1979, but the 21st century," Arya points out as he waits for the seemingly endless upload. "They won't get away with this coup d'état."

You may be wondering how the country's Internet surfers will cope without access to their usual means of news and communication, but there is no need to worry too much as a number of Iranian sites based overseas are working to help keep them connected through foreign servers, at the same time sidestepping the censorship issue. This technique works, but is painfully slow.

"Some people spend hours uploading the same video," Arya laughs. "And that's *before* you even take into account the fact that your connection could drop at any second, sending you right back to the beginning. That's the price you pay for freedom, I guess."

At the end of this noble effort, videos are sent via email to BBC Persian, Voice of America, CNN, and France24, their addresses posted on Twitter, Facebook, Yahoo! and Google Chat. From there they are taken up by the Iranian diaspora in the West, who in turn busy themselves with the wider distribution.

"This is Iran, not Afghanistan," Arya reminds us with a smile. "Our parents organized the revolution in 1979? We organized the revolution 2.0."

For once, the people are not alone in this venture. After the results were announced, the defeated candidate Mir-Hossein Mousavi had two choices. He could quietly accept Supreme Leader Ayatollah Khamenei's decision to uphold the election results and thus be reduced to a "nobody" in the eyes of his people, just like the former reformist President Khatami before him when he condemned the 1999 student demonstrations. Or he could stand up to this injustice and, by extension, to the ruling authority of his country, stepping once again into his hero shoes.

Rumors are circulating around Omid that the reformer is giving a speech with the help of a half-broken loudspeaker attached to his old truck.

"I will not surrender to this dangerous charade," he famously stated. "You must stand up against this government of lies and tyranny. I am ready to pay the price for it." In thirty years of the Islamic Republic, a member of the regime has never been so bold. "These crowds were not bussed in from afar, they did not come here under threat,"[1] he added. "They are not here for potatoes. They came here themselves."

"*Damesh garm*," Omid cries from the crowd. "At least he's got guts."

In this same manner, the other defeated candidate Mehdi Karoubi, along with former reformist President Khatami, could be spotted, perched on the roof of their vehicle.

"The sons of this regime are taking a stand," Azadeh smiles.

As further proof of this statement, candidate Mohsen Rezaï, who, as former head of the paramilitary force, the Revolutionary Guard, carries considerable weight himself, also took great issue with the results. In a statement which spoke to the consensus of the Iranian clergy, Grand Ayatollah Sanei, one of the country's highest religious authorities, declared that any Muslim cooperating with Ahmadinejad or his supporters would be guilty of *haram*, of a mortal sin. And following in these footsteps, even Supreme Leader Ayatollah Khamenei, Iran's true head of state, having previously described Ahmadinejad's reelection as a "crushing victory" and "divine blessing," turned on his heels and, in an unexpected announcement, authorized Mousavi to contest the results "within the legal system." Among other things, Khamenei requested that the Guardian Council of the Constitution, the powerful body put in place to supervise the election, investigate the accusations of fraud put forward by the reformist.

"We'll get there in the end," Azadeh is optimistic. "Nothing can stop us now. Nothing will ever be the same again."

Three hours later, as the sun goes down on Azadi Square, tens of thousands of protesters, including Azadeh and Omid, have already headed home, anxious to relay the historic events to their families. Kian, the sentimental guitarist, is still here, arm in arm with thousands of his fellow men and women, savoring this rare feeling of peace.

"I told you, my people would want to get together, to enjoy this moment," the musician sighs. "Look, there are millions of them here today. Only Iranians would do this kind of thing."

Before long, however, a terrible rumor catches up with the gathering. According to a number of students present this evening, the University of Tehran dormitories were raided the night before. Dozens of students were arrested and many others were killed, some thrown from windows.

"They're crazy," Kian cries. "What the hell did they do to deserve that?"

As the night sky grows darker, those pleasant feelings of innocence which reigned throughout the day now make way for tension and fear. North of Freedom Square, Jenah Street houses barracks for the Basiji militia. Around ten officers are stationed on the roof; blue shirts, black protection masks, and most noticeable of all, Kalashnikovs at their sides.

"Sons of bitches. Infidels!" they scream at the top of their lungs. "You thought you could take down our revolution like that? God help you all."

Kian is afraid. He and his fellow protesters greatly outnumber the militiamen tonight, but these are the same people who have been violating his rights on a daily basis for as long as he can remember. The same people who constantly harass him because of his clothes or hairstyle, who gate-crash his parties, confiscate his car and his instruments, and hound his girlfriend, all under a shield of impunity.

"Basijis, shame on you. Let the people be free," shouts a nearby woman dressed in a black chador, her cry quickly echoed by Kian, his bandmates, and before long, the entire group of protesters. It is a beautiful sight, a crowd of individuals united as one. Sick and tired of this public hostility, one of the militiamen, a guy by the name of Satar, reaches for his weapon and fires . . . with real bullets.

"Get down, get down!" the crowd panics.

Fortunately, these were just shots in the air, and the militiaman's actions are met with boos from the crowd, some of whom throw stones while others begin to chant again.

"Basiji, shame on you. Let the people be free."

Furious now, they go for their weapons a second time, only this time they aim directly at the protesters.

"Get down, get down!"

The firing ceases, and the crowd can finally get back to its feet. One man, however, remains on the ground, writhing in agony.

"Bastards, they really fired," murmurs float over the crowd. The scene is reminiscent of a PlayStation 3 shoot-'em-up game, except that no one can possibly deny that this is anything but cruel, cold reality. The bleeding body stops moving.

"He's dead, they killed him," people scream as panic sets in. Some begin to make their escape while another group lifts the body up to the skies, a throwback to the darkest hours of the 1979 revolution.

"I'll kill him, I'll kill the man who killed my brother," they cry at the tops of their lungs. Unmoved, the militants watch as the crowd works itself up into a frenzy. The protesters are furious.

"This time they're finally going to pay for thirty years of misery," Kian shouts.

A determined group of around fifty demonstrators rushes toward the barracks, chanting with arms in the air.

"Death to the dictator. Death to the dictator."

Minutes later and the building is alight; a plume of thick, black smoke rising up into Tehran's night sky. Another Basiji officer, still stationed at his post on the roof, lifts up his weapon again, this time not stopping until each and every bullet has been used. Below, the slogans are silenced. The crowd is on the ground, heads between their knees, waiting for the ordeal to be over. Seconds feel like hours as bullets rain down without reprieve. A few seconds later, things seem to have returned to normal, but many do not get back up.

"Stop this carnage, don't you have any mercy?" screams Kian, who witnessed the entire scene before finally making a run for it. "If they've got nothing to hide over this election, then why are they killing us?"

"I'll kill him, I'll kill the man who killed my brother," the crowd starts up again. This day, which began in a cloud of peace, innocence, and good cheer, ends in a shroud of horror and fear.

The following morning, Payam, the state radio station, will announce that seven people were killed and many others injured as "hooligans attacked a military post and vandalized public property." These announcements, however, are not enough to prevent Omid, Azadeh, and Kian from taking to the streets again in silence the following day, this time in Toopkhaneh Square, in the south of the city, to peacefully demand a new vote.

12

CRASHED OUT ON THE COUCH, Mandana and her daughter Azadeh cannot take the nail-biting anymore and move on to a bowl of pistachios. A day has passed since they learned of the murder of around ten protesters, and Mandana's eyes are still wet with tears.

"*Khodaya* [Oh my God]. I'd give my own life for them if I could. It hurts as if they were my own children. Does this regime really have no pity for its young ones?" She goes on, "My girl, you'll keep on going out there, you understand? Starting tomorrow." She looks her daughter straight in the eye, causing a wide smile to creep across the girl's face. This afternoon, the people of Iran are taking a break, or at least a brief time-out. For just ninety minutes, they can forget the crisis currently engulfing their country. Today is the day that Team Melli, Iran's national soccer team, will play their last World Cup qualifying match in South Korea, their final chance of making it to South Africa 2010. If they lose this one, they risk elimination.

"These kids just want to make us happy, to make us proud," says Mandana. "And boy do we need it right now."

The people of Iran have long suffered from the well-known disease that is soccer fever. For the country's men, this sport offers a rare opportunity to enjoy themselves and let loose, albeit vicariously, through a hobby or activity. They are not alone in this, for their women have been carried along on this wave as well, swooning for the young players on the team whose names and numbers they know by heart. The players' stardom is also largely due to their roles of ambassadors to the Iranian people, to their image as Persian soldiers, which have been assigned to them by their fans. Ali Karimi, nicknamed the "Maradona of Asia," and Mehdi Mahdavikia, the talented and *khoshtip* (good-looking) captain, have already moved on to play for such teams as Bayern Munich and Hamburg.

"The amazing thing is that they're really just little kids from the streets of South Tehran," Azadeh explains in admiration.

Iranian women are forbidden from even entering a stadium, the reason being that to delight in the spectacle of a group of men running around in shorts, in the boisterous environment of a stadium, would be in direct contrast to the teachings of Islam. Four years ago, however, Azadeh and a group of feminist friends managed to sweet-talk the authorities—not without difficulty—into allowing them to purchase tickets to Iran's match against Bahrain during the 2006 World Cup qualifiers.

"When Iranian women want something, they find a way to get it," she laughs. As the final whistle blew, Iran had made it to the next stage, and millions of Iranians descended into the streets to celebrate as they had always dreamed, strutting their stuff with headscarves in the air. "That night, there was no Islamic Republic," she remembers, as if in a dream.

Fast-forward to today: after four years of Ahmadinejad, one stolen election, and many deaths in the streets of the capital, it is clear that this match could not have come at a better time.

One day off will not hurt the cause too much, and as the game kicks off on televisions around the country, the streets of the capital are empty. After the customary pregame lineup presentation, the live action begins.

"*Iran sourakhesh mikoneh* [Iran will rip their nets to shreds]," Mandana cries.

Ali Karimi, the people's idol, kicks off, but after a series of impressive dribbles, is tackled to the ground down by a Korean opponent. As the camera zooms in for a close-up of the young player rolling around on the ground, a tiny detail catches Azadeh's eye.

"Mom . . . Mom, check it out! Look what he has around his wrist."

"You've got to be kidding me," Mandana reacts in turn, a heavy tear running down her round cheek. "God almighty, he's wearing a green ribbon . . . this little kid from some neighborhood in the south is wearing a green ribbon around his wrist!" Bursting into tears, she falls into her daughter's arms and they sob together.

"*Damesh garm*," is the cry from Omid, who is also in a state of utter disbelief.

"*Eyval, Karimi, eyval. Eyval, Karimi, eyval* [Bravo, Karimi, bravo]," his friends, gathered at his place to watch the game, begin to sing.

It is not only the Iranian team's star who has decided to defy the government on this important day; no less than five other players, some of whom are well-known household names, have also donned the famous ribbons. They include Hossein Kaabi, Vahid Hashemian, Javad Nekounam, and most importantly, team captain Mehdi Mahdavikia, who as a point of honor has also chosen to wear a green colored captain's armband. This move is an extremely bold one, considering how the Islamic Republic treats members of the resistance—regardless of popularity status—but on top of that, these players must remember that they will be returning to Tehran the very next day. Perhaps they have decided that to warm the hearts of seventy million Iranians at this moment is worth all the risks in the world.

"I am his servant. I am his father's servant, his mother's servant, and his grandmother's servant"[1] Kian shouts from his basement, his music and his disillusions placed on the back burner for just ninety minutes.

In Seoul, it is not only the players who are showing their support for the opposition movement. Before the match, dozens of supporters, dressed in green, staged a miniprotest outside the stadium. From the very first few minutes of the game, they waved *Death to the Dictator* banners from the stands, held placards reading *Free Iran*, and altered the words of their traditional chants, singing "Compatriots, we will be with you until the end, with the same hearts."

The effect was such that Iranian state television, whose live broadcasts are transmitted with a delay of several seconds, was forced to reduce the volume in a bid to drown out the slogans as much as possible.

The Koreans now have the ball, and this time it is Ali Karimi's turn to unleash a ferocious tackle on his opponent. The Iranian player rushes immediately toward the referee, arms in the air as a sign of innocence, offering the video cameras the perfect opportunity to zoom in on his wrists.

Azadeh cracks up laughing. "He's crazy . . . he knows full well that if he does that, the camera will pick up on the ribbon around his wrist."

His number 7 jersey soaked through and transparent with sweat, it is impossible to miss the T-shirt he wears underneath, on which the green print clearly reads *Iran*. "Oh God, let him score," his young fan prays. "I beg you."

The halftime whistle blows and Omid and his friends step out to get a melon juice. In the neighborhood, people can talk of nothing but the match, and not because they wish to critique the team's performance, as would often be the case.

"*Mashallah* to each one of these children," Bahman, an elderly neighbor, is emotional. "They are the ones who will save this country."

"If they step foot back in Iran, it's all over for them," Pedram, a friend, adds. Whether he knows it or not, the young man never said a truer word.

As they take to the field for the second half, not a single player still sports a green ribbon, with the exception of Mehdi Mahdavikia, who is obliged to wear his captain's arm band throughout the match. "They must have really got in some serious trouble in the locker room," Omid guesses.

After opening the scoring with all the excitement of a World Cup final, the Koreans finally equalize and Iran can wave good-bye to the Cup. Their people will not receive the gift they were hoping for, another consequence of the fact that the technical talent of these young individuals is wasted due to inadequate coaching back at home. But while they may have to forget South Africa and the giant party of which they had dreamed, there is not one home in Iran this evening which is not beaming with pride for its "children."

"They have given us, the Iranian people, the most beautiful gift we could have dreamed of," Mandana sobs. "That's worth all the Cups in the world."

Unfortunately, on their return to the Islamic Republic, the players, like the protesters before them, must pay the price for their actions. Victims of the government's zero tolerance, Team Melli's four best players, Ali Karimi, captain Mehdi Mahdavikia, Vahid Hashemian, and Hossein Kaabi (just twenty-four years old) will have their passports confiscated and be forced into "retirement." Embarrassed by the affair, Mansour Pourheidari, the team's chief administrator, will later explain that the green ribbons were in fact worn in homage to Imam Hossein, in the hope of bringing a victory to Iran.

13

*T*ODAY IS A BIG DAY. One of those days that defines the history of a country, of a population, or of a regime. At midday on Friday, June 19, seventy million Iranians are again glued to the TV screens in their homes, only this time it is not for a soccer match. One long, volatile week after Mahmoud Ahmadinejad was reelected as president, Supreme Leader Ayatollah Khamenei, the country's highest-ranking political and religious authority, is to take to the stage and speak to the nation during Friday prayers. This speech is long-awaited, especially after the leader's sudden about-face at the beginning of the week, originally confirming the results before then going back on his decision, sending out massive ripples of hope among the population.

"Today we're going to get this thing sorted out," Arya explains, alone in his now-empty office. "Either the leader is on our side and will announce his support for a new election, in which case we are on our way to a peaceful resolution to this crisis, or he's going to come out against the demonstrators and then we're going to see this situation get a lot more serious."

Sitting at her mother's side, Azadeh is more optimistic, giddy, even, with excitement. "This is a historic day," she grins. "Khamenei is about to stand by the people for the first time in his life. There's no other choice, if he doesn't want to fuel the population's anger against the regime." The young woman has it all planned out. "Once the powers that be go back on this election, they will be forced to go back on a whole bunch of other reforms. In the long term, it means that the Islamic Republic is doomed."

Mandana, who has seen enough disappointments in her time, is more prudent and does not share her daughter's optimistic opinion. "I was just like you, my girl, I didn't believe at the time that the regime could possibly last another year. But you don't know just how many people they killed in order to stay in power. You don't know them, but I do."

This last statement enrages Azadeh. "I don't know them? Is that supposed to be a joke? Which one of us was born into the arms of the Islamic Republic? Who is it that has ruined my life and all of that because of your stupid revolution? At least you and your friends had fun in your twenties." Mandana hangs her head and does not reply.

Finally, the supreme leader's arrival is announced. Huge crowds have been packed into the university, with many more gathered outside.

"*Allahu Akbar. Khamenei Rahbar* [God is great. Khamenei is our leader]," they chant mechanically before striking up a loop of the legendary 1979 favorites: "Death to America" and "Death to Israel."

Banners are waved; "Don't let foreign pens write the history of Iran" is but one example. According to state television reports, "thousands upon thousands" of people are present today, showing their support for the supreme leader and, by extension, the Islamic Republic.

"Of course they are," Arya sniggers. "These people are the regime's core, traditional 'members.' It's the Basijis, the people from the provinces who've been paid to be here, the civil servants here under force."

In any case, the leader seems unfazed by the excitement, obviously used to such levels of spontaneous support. The extent of it this time, however, is such that he has to make several attempts before he can begin his speech. He thanks his audience, including the newly reelected president, and mutters a few prayers in Arabic before continuing.

"At the June 12 election, we witnessed an enormous display of the willingness of our people to participate in deciding its future. We saw proof of the love those people hold for this regime. No other country can boast such levels of democracy . . . It is the first time that we have seen such levels of participation since the revolution. The younger generation, in particular, showed that it takes an interest in such matters and proved itself to be acutely political."

Sitting directly in front of her screen, Azadeh does not know whether she should laugh or cry. "You hear that, Mom? I'm in love with the regime. Well, it's the first time I've ever fallen in love . . . don't you think I could have found someone a bit better looking?" Her smile quickly fades. "We've been tricked again, why did I even bother to vote? Why did I try to trust this system again?" Her mother sits with her head in her hands as her daughter continues to rant. "No, really, that's it. I don't believe in anything anymore. I'll never vote again."

Meanwhile, the leader continues his explanation. "Of course there are differences of opinion within the population. Some would have preferred to see their candidate come out on top, that's only natural. This election was a great celebration of the revolution, in which every person showed their love and their loyalty."

"The bastards," Omid screams from the comfort of his living room. "I knew that those twenty days of 'celebration' would come at a price. Now they're turning them around, using them for their cause. It makes me sick."

"This election was a religious, democratic event," the leader continues. "It has sent the message to countries living under dictatorship that we are a religious democracy."

"Democracy and religion," Mandana groans. "They act as if those two words were compatible."

"This election has also shown that the people of this country are full of conviction, hope, and joy. Our enemies have tried to exploit that."

"Enemies?" Azadeh shouts suddenly. "I'm sick of their 'enemies.'" For thirty years of the Islamic Republic, the word has been used liberally to describe the Americans and Israelis. "The only enemy here is Ahmadinejad," the young woman concludes.

"But if our young people had not felt free, then they would never even have participated in this election. The trust they put in the Islamic Republic is its greatest asset," Ayatollah Khamenei now delivers this harsh blow.

Alone in his office, Arya smashes the lead in his pencil as he strikes the table violently. "That's it, the trap is closing in on us now." He is dismayed. "This doesn't look good. And to think that I called people out to vote . . ."

"There have been accusations of fraud, even before the election took place. Pay no attention: the contest was transparent. Our enemies, along with the evil Zionists, tried to expose the election as a fight between advocates and opponents of the regime. This is not true. Each candidate supports the regime . . . Each of the candidates is part of the system and part of the regime." So the leader would have it.

"This is exactly what I said would happen, right from the beginning," Omid sniggers as he enjoys a succulent *chelo-kabab* (skewered lamb with rice). "Once again the people of Iran got all excited, and for nothing. I was right not to vote."

The elderly man continues his speech. "The Zionists, along with British radio, announced that this election debate threw into question the very existence of the regime. But this was an internal debate, happening within the system, and was in no means against the revolution."

"That is probably the only true word he will say today," Azadeh smiles as the leader goes on.

"The dispute was between the candidates themselves, and there were as many pros as there were cons. We gave the people the right to judge, for they too are part of the system. Every different point of view was available to the people and the result was clear. They chose the candidates they wished for."

The room's ceiling shakes with the force of Arya's fist as it slams down onto his desk. "What? The candidates they wished for? Mr. Leader, is your memory failing you? Have you forgotten the 471 candidates, forty-two of them women, who were turned down by the Guardian Council of the Constitution?"

According to the ayatollah, "the candidate debates reached as far as the streets and the houses of the people. This strengthens the system and should not be misinterpreted . . . False rumors have been going around and have given the previous government a bad image. Who really believes that it is acceptable to call the president a liar when this is simply untrue? Thirty years of revolution have been tarnished."

"With respect," Arya interjects, "it was *your* candidates who threw accusations at each other during the programs that you yourself organized. All the people did was watch."

Khamenei continues. "The president's opinions are closest to my own . . . The people chose who they wanted."

"Well, there you go," Arya says again. "You could have just said that from the start."

"We don't pretend that there is no corruption within our regime," Khamenei goes on to say. Omid, shocked, has put down his spoonful of rice and stopped chewing. For the first time in his life, he is listening to the highest authority in the country admit that there is corruption within the Islamic Republic. "But it is still one of the healthiest systems in the world. And the Zionist's corruption accusations are false."

Omid almost chokes from laughing. "Leave the Zionists alone," he chuckles.

"My dear people, June 12 marked a historic event. Our enemies wanted to cast doubt on it and make it look as if the regime had been defeated . . . But the people have faith in the revolution and in the Republic. The Islamic Republic plays tricks on nobody. There is no fraud within the electoral system. It is carefully monitored and controlled. The president was elected with twenty-four million votes. Perhaps there are a few errors here and there, but there is no way that there were eleven million of them. How could you possibly cheat with such a margin?"

Now it is Azadeh's turn to chuckle, but her laugh is forced. "Now I've seen everything. There has been some fraud . . . but not enough to invalidate the election."

"The Guardian Council, however, has announced that if the people have their doubts, then they must prove it," the elderly man concedes. "I will not pursue false allegations. Every election has its winners and its losers. Appropriate legal procedures must be followed in order to ensure trust in the system."

"Well, there we have it." Arya despairs. "I'm sure we'll get really far with a Guardian Council and a judicial system dominated by conservatives."

Now comes the warning. "The candidates should be wary of what they say and do. Political leaders who have an influence over the people should pay very careful attention to how they behave. If they act in an extremist manner, this extremism will reach a point of no return . . . they will be responsible for bloodshed, violence, and chaos."

Arya swallows with difficulty. "The stakes are clear," he summarizes. "Either the two candidates keep quiet and it's all over, or they continue and it's prison for them and a bloodbath for us."

"The streets are a place of life and of exchange. Why do you take over our streets? Arm wrestling in the streets is a mistake, and I want it to end . . . I will not give up the streets. Truth comes from the ballot box, not from the street." Rubbing salt into the wound, the supreme leader has just definitively confirmed the results. Azadeh is aghast.

Still he goes on. "These protests are tantamount to extremism, people have been killed . . . The protests are perfect places for terrorist plots . . . We see these elements attacking those that support the Islamic Republic . . . Who will be responsible if the same thing happens to *them*? As you know, I am just one poor soul . . ." The crowd sheds tears, an image zoomed in on and blown up by the cameras.

"Give me a break," Mandana laughs. "He thinks he's our father or something? And all of this stuff about terrorist plots . . . Is he calling the Basijis terrorists?"

The speaker moves now to giving out orders. "Protesting after an election is not a solution. It only throws elections into question."

"Well done. He's a smart one, isn't he?" Azadeh smiles.

"If they continue, then they'll only get what they deserve."

The young woman is not smiling anymore. The message is loud and clear. She falls into her mother's arms and sobs once again.

Enough with the orders; the time has come for the threats. "If they continue, there will be other, behind-the-scenes consequences. I ask my friends and my brothers to obey these laws. May God help you follow the right path. May God bless you all."

"Leave God out of this," Mandana exclaims, still comforting her distraught daughter. "You've been persecuting in his name for thirty years now."

Game over. The nation is stunned. Those that were counting on an offer of compromise from the leader know now what they can expect. There will be no concessions. Ayatollah Khamenei has decided to stand heart and soul behind his little lamb Ahmadinejad, even if it means putting the regime in danger. From now on, any new protests will be met with a fierce response from the authorities. This is particularly worrying in light of the fact that the opposition have called for new demonstrations, set to start tomorrow.

14

"MY DEAR CHILDREN, my soldiers of Islam, the future of the Islamic Republic is in your hands today," Hamid announces sternly to a group of Basijis in the Valiasr Street station. As dawn breaks over Tehran, Javad and fifty other members of the militia listen carefully to the orders of their superior.

"Today is a crucial day for the future of your country. As you all heard yesterday, our almighty leader has definitively confirmed the election results."

"*Allahu Akbar. Khamenei Rahbar,*" the militiamen chant in response.

Raising his voice, their boss continues. "A group of infidels, of mercenaries employed by our Zionist enemies, has decided to plunge our country into a pit of fire and blood. Do not let yourselves be fooled by their appearance. They may be young, they may be old, they may even be dressed in women's chadors, but they have been sent from overseas to set light to our mosques and to rape our mothers and our sisters."

"No way." Javad is suddenly overcome with excitement. "We must protect our country from these devils."

A nod of agreement from Hamid, who goes on. "Look back at what happened last Monday. Remember the young satanists and unveiled women who took over our streets. Is that what you want to see happen to our country?"

"Never," they vow in chorus.

"Don't bury your heads in the sand and don't listen to these hypocrites, for they are not your friends. These are the same people who curse you on a daily basis. If the traitor Mousavi is ever in power, you will no longer exist."

"Death to Mousavi. Death to Mousavi," the young men sing at the top of their lungs.

"This election was just a pretext for them. Over twenty-four million of our fellow men voted for Ahmadinejad and they dare to question the result. Our beloved leader announced yesterday that he would not stand for any more riots, but despite this, some still plan to take to the streets in defiance of his words."

"Basijis are not afraid to die, they will not stand for oppression." The chant comes from one of the men and is quickly echoed by the entire station, proof that it is not only the opposition who enjoy inventing *shoar* for their cause.

"Don't worry," Hamid continues. "You are not alone. This time around we have prepared and today there will be *gardeh vijeh* [special antiriot police force] in place around the city. The leader, however, is counting on you personally to enforce his decision. You play a vital role. *Allahu Akbar.*"

"*Allahu Akbar,*" the militiamen repeat in unison, their cries resonating around the neighborhood. Fifteen of today's militiamen are given Kalashnikovs whereas others leave armed with a sniper. As for Javad, he has a revolver carefully tucked into his pants.

"Don't forget, my children, you are God's soldiers."

Today, rather than enforcing the law from the rooftop of their station, the young Basijis will be mounted on 250cc motocross bikes, currently banned within the country.

"Whatever you do, don't stop," Hamid warns. "They'll be all over you. The idea is to frighten them to the max and, if you have to, don't hesitate to shoot. You have the blessing of our almighty leader. This act will be considered *halal* [blessed], and you will be compensated."

Javad's eyes light up. The leader has already been kind today, promising the equivalent of $425 for the day's work and an extra $200 for every protester they successfully identify. Generosity indeed, and all that before we even mention the tens of sublime virgins waiting for them in heaven.

Not all of the Basijis will be operating on bikes today, as Hamid explains. "Some of you will be taking part in a much more high-risk, important operation. It will be your job to outsmart the enemy."

Among the young people assigned this perilous task is twenty-one-year-old Reza. He is not wearing a helmet, a uniform, or even a beard but is dressed instead in a tight checked shirt, carefully tucked into faded jeans, a style which has earned him the nickname *khareji* (foreigner) among his peers. His jeans, however, are the hiding place for a much more sinister object: a kitchen knife which he has personally sharpened.

Their marching orders have been given, and the militiamen set off.

"*Allahu Akbar,*" they shout to psych themselves up for the fight to come. Many of them, their adolescence not far behind them, are already trembling.

"*Allahu Akbar,*" the same cry comes from the large crowds which line Kargar Street, not far from Enghelab Square. As predicted, Iranians of all ages and classes have ignored the recommendations of their leader and taken to the streets in great numbers. The special police forces have already asserted a significant presence in the square, preventing protesters from gathering and forcing them into neighboring streets. Seated comfortably on his motorbike about fifty feet from the square, Javad looks surprised; he was not expecting to see such crowds and is particularly struck by the sight of a grandmother accompanying her grandchildren.

"*Allahu Akbar!*" he screams, the leader's words flooding back to him. "Infidels, how dare you? You who want to abolish Islam . . . are you really that hypocritical?"

Around fifty motorbikes from various stations around the capital have converged at this one point. At the head of the procession is thirty-year-old Morteza, with a thick beard and a large stomach, which bulges from his open shirt. "All right kids, you haven't forgotten your orders? Let's go, it's our turn to play now. We're going to save our country."

He waves his arm as a starting signal, and they set off. The driver launches into first gear as Javad clings to him from behind to prevent himself from falling, his revolver in the other hand. The move has its desired effect and sends the crowd scrambling in all directions to get out of the way.

"Run, the Basijis are coming," they cry, sending a strange smile across Javad's face. He is on top of the world, the new *shah* (king) of the street. Carried away with this feeling of power, he fires several shots into the air as proof.

"God help you, you fucking infidels!" It could be mistaken for a scene straight out of a *Mad Max* movie, but this is a far cry from Hollywood.

Farther down the road, the crowd is not ready to give in quite so easily.

"Death to the dictator!" They direct their cries at Ahmadinejad, or perhaps even at Ayatollah Khamenei. Among the protesters is a young stylish man with a baby face. He waves his arms as if he were at a soccer match, seemingly to catch the attention of his peers.

Suddenly he begins to cry, "Death to Khamenei. Death to Khamenei."

A long silence follows as dozens of protesters turn to stare at him, the first person in thirty years of the Islamic Republic to dare to utter these taboo words. Without a shadow of a doubt, punishment for such an infraction would be the death penalty.

"He's right, *baba*," one elderly man breaks the silence. "Death to Khamenei."

These three words are slowly taken up by the rest of the crowd who, distracted as they are by the adrenaline that comes from such risk-taking, do not notice as a young man steps directly behind the young protester, a boy who cannot be much older than he is. As the crowd moves back and forth, he takes his opportunity, pulls out his knife, and stabs the boy straight through the heart. The young protester drops to the ground as Reza quietly slips away.

A little farther down, another young man, whose slogans are targeted at Ahmadinejad himself, is jumped by half a dozen Basijis as they defend their president.

"Filthy mercenary. You tell your Western friends that this is how we'll welcome them if they invade our country." He is thrown to the ground, beaten with a billy club, and kicked from all sides as dozens of protesters rush to defend him. Bombarded with stones, the militiamen have no choice but to flee the scene.

"Our brothers are under attack," Javad screams as he and a group of twenty fellow officers, alerted on their walkie-talkies, rush to the site. Never one to miss an opportunity, he swings at people with his bat as they fly past. Given the speed of the motorbike, his billy club acts more like a sword, and many protesters are left with huge gashes and cuts. Javad does not even look back. When they arrive at the scene, the vigilantes surround the stone-throwers, firing in the air, and forcing them into an adjacent alley with their billy clubs, a technique which has been drilled into them by Hamid. Once they succeed in isolating the core group of protesters, the militiamen avenge their friends. Six shots are fired; then it is back into first gear as the young men take off as quickly as they arrived.

Night falls over the Valiasr station. Javad parks his motorbike and rejoins his fellow fighters, a smile stretching across his face.

"Congratulations, boys," Hamid exclaims, offering a prayer in Arabic. "*Allahu Akbar*. You managed to push back the enemy. Our supreme leader is proud of you."

"*Allahu Akbar*," they respond, proud of themselves but exhausted. A good number of them are now wearing bloodstained shirts. Hamid opens the station refrigerator and breaks out a box of vanilla and chocolate Häagen-Dazs ice creams.

"Help yourselves, kids. You deserve it." It is a modest gift to compensate a long, hard day of work. "Today, over a hundred of our enemy were defeated, thanks to you," their boss announces proudly.

"I'm the happiest man in the world," Javad thinks to himself.

Before heading home for the night, each young man stops into Hamid's office. Javad does as the others and finds six $100 traveler's checks waiting for him.

"Here you go, *azizam* [my dear]. You defended yourself like a lion today. I hope that this small blessing will help your family." Hamid puts his arm around the young man who, despite his pride and satisfaction, cannot help but feel a little envious. Reza, with his knife covered in blood, went home tonight with nine traveler's checks in his pocket.

15

"*ALLAHU AKBAR*," a large group of protesters cries at the top of their lungs as they make their way down Azadi Street. Just one day after Ayatollah Khamenei's speech, could it possibly be that these Iranians have finally decided to pledge allegiance to their supreme leader?

"I'd rather die," Kian smiles, a green scarf hanging around his neck. "It's just that this is the only way we've found to stop ourselves from getting killed."

It was Imam Khomeini, founder of the Islamic Republic, who encouraged his people in 1979 to chant this slogan against the Shah as a symbol of the clergy's power.

"Today," the guitarist continues, "it's the only way to keep a brave face on things and to ensure that we are safe. And don't forget, just because we don't believe in their Islam, it doesn't mean we don't believe in God . . . *Allahu Akbar.*"

Today's protests will draw tens of thousands of people, in groups dispersed around the capital, a number far below the millions seen on Monday. It could be that yesterday's speech did have some impact after all.

The special police forces are certainly asserting more of a presence than at the beginning of the week, and all access to Azadi and Enghelab Squares, principal meeting points for the protests, have been cut off. At each surrounding junction there are dozens of regular police officers, as well as militiamen and special police forces, all keeping a close eye on the situation and randomly setting upon anyone who stops or upon any group of more than two individuals.

"Apparently, there are Basijis on motorbikes every fifteen feet," Kian explains. "I've never seen a siege quite like it."

Despite this, the protesters defy their leader by taking to the adjacent streets leading to the two famous squares, accepting the risk that they may run into the wrong kind of people in these less-open spaces.

They have the support of two noteworthy people today, the first of whom, Mir-Hossein Mousavi, is in attendance himself, announcing that he is ready to "die a martyr." The second, Grand Ayatollah Montazeri, one of the most prestigious figures in Shiite Islam and once believed to be Imam Khomeini's successor as supreme leader, has written a letter of support to the protesters in an unprecedented move. In this letter he denounces the results which, according to him, "no one in their right mind could believe," and which show "every sign of manipulation." He goes on to state that any "government that does not respect its people's vote has no religious or political legitimacy."

"Don't be afraid, don't be afraid. We have each other," the crowd of protesters chants. There are dozens of them: young men in jeans and running shoes, students coming back from class, and mothers in headscarves, all walking arm in arm down this narrow Tehran alleyway. While fear is ever-present at the event, the general atmosphere is remarkably relaxed. A few young men amuse themselves with the most recent joke about the Basijis and their "wooden dicks," sending ripples of laughter through the crowd.

Kian, spotting an elderly lady among the demonstrators, cries out, "Bravo, Grandma, I didn't know that Iranian women were so brave."

"What on earth did you think, my dear?" she smiles. "We're the ones who put them where they are today, so we're the ones who will get rid of them for you."

Despite the number of deaths this week, Kian seems to be in good spirits. "It's just amazing. Never in my life have I seen the Iranian people pulling together like this, but to think that it took such atrocities to make it happen . . ."

Along the way, the street's inhabitants film the scene from their windows. "You up there, 'honorable Iranians,' come and support us . . . come and support us!" the protesters shout in their direction. A few minutes later, around thirty special police agents, the infamous *gardeh vijeh* in their Robocop uniforms, tear through the alleyway, smashing cars, windows, and everything else in their path. Tense looks are ex-changed.

"Don't be afraid, don't be afraid. We have each other," the protest-ers start up again, even louder this time with men and women chanting together. Car alarms are going off all around. *"Allahu Akbar. Allahu Akbar,"* they try to reassure themselves and each other.

All of a sudden, grenades come flying toward the demonstrators, immediately unleashing tear gas among the group. "Close your eyes, cover your face," Kian cries.

Women use their headscarves as protection, while others had pre-pared for this eventuality and are armed with sunglasses and surgical masks. The attack is in full swing, and as many escape into neighboring alleyways, one young man gets caught up in the crowd and falls. Two officers are quickly upon him, beating him from all sides with their feet and billy clubs, neglecting to consider whether he had actually posed a threat to them at all. When his attackers look up, they are confronted by a crowd of twenty furious protesters, at the head of which are several women, brandishing their purses as weapons.

"You bastards," they cry in shrill voices. The attackers have no choice but to abandon their prey as they make a run for it. The pro-testers jump for joy in all directions, dispersing the cloud of fear once again.

A little farther down the scene can only be described as that of war. Thick gray smoke pours from Shadmehr Street, stones and debris are strewn all around, and women cry, "Death to the dicta-tor. Death to the dictator." Azadeh and Mandana are at this par-ticular gathering, unfazed by the direct threats made by the supreme leader.

"Khodaya," they whimper together. "May they not turn their weapons against their fellow men. In the name of God, Mercy, and the Almighty," they begin to pray. This mother-daughter duo faces covered to prevent identification, are busy gathering stones from the gutter to hand to their male counterparts. These stones are then hurled in the direction of the Basiji militiamen, stationed fifty feet away, to force them to back up.

"*Afarin* [Bravo]. *Mashallah* [Congratulations]," their neighbors egg the women on. A woman in a black chador struggles to form a barricade by dragging a heavy trash can across the street. Three men quickly jump to assist her, then put their arms around her as they chant, "Grandma, we love you. Grandma, we love you," a slogan quickly adopted by the crowd. The young men wave their V for victory finger signs at the militiamen before setting light to the trash can with government newspapers in a bid to scare off their aggressors.

Azadeh and her mother applaud as the young people start up again. "Until Ahmadinejad goes, every day will be like this."

Suddenly, the Tehran night sky is filled with the sound of gunshots. First one then two, and soon a whole series of them. "Don't worry, Mom," Azadeh is excited. "All they're trying to do is scare us, and besides, they're only using rubber bullets anyway."

After exchange brief glances, they continue to march forward, but new rounds of shots cause the crowd to look to one another once more for how to proceed.

"Watch out, kids. Hey! There are Basijis on the rooftops," a man cries from his window. The effort is a wasted one as the protesters cannot hear him over the two helicopters roaring through the sky above them.

"*Allahu Akbar!*" They prefer to strike up another call as they hold hands for support. Two young men, evidently having the time of their lives, lead the way, waving their arms around like a pair of soccer fans. Another round of shots rings out and the two fall to the ground, their T-shirts covered in blood. The teenage corpses are picked up and carried toward the crowd. Witnessing this scene, the protesters finally understand.

"*Khodaya* [Oh my God]. They're killing, they're actually killing!" they shout themselves hoarse.

"Bastards, mercenaries, infidels. Run, everyone, run . . ." come the cries from farther down. The crowd rushes into neighboring alleyways, a few holding up cell phones to film the victims. Surrounding the bodies, a dozen protesters cry over and over again as a sign of protest, "*Allahu Akbar. Allahu Akbar.*"

Azadeh grabs her mother's hand and dives into a narrow street. The neighbors, who witnessed the entire scene from above, rush to their doors to let them in, to shelter them from the approaching militiamen. A dozen protesters make it into the refuge of one particular house in this western neighborhood of Tehran, cramming through the door before their host locks the entrance grille behind them. Azadeh and her mother are in tears and fall into the arms of their savior, a woman in her fifties who pleads with them to make as little noise as possible. The television is on. The Islamic Republic is thanking its people for not taking to the streets today.

"Assholes . . . they'll pay for this," the woman exclaims. Across from her, behind the grille, a number of protesters remain trapped. The special police forces have finally reached the street and are greeted by cries from neighboring rooftops.

"Leave them alone."

"You call yourselves Iranians?"

"Even the Israelis aren't this cruel."

A number of demonstrators are handcuffed, and the trucks start up. Ten minutes later, all is calm again in the street—no traces of protesters, no bloody corpses glistening in the sun.

In Tohid Square, however, blood still runs through the gutters. A dozen lifeless bodies are laid out on the ground as bullets rain down from above.

"It's a battlefield here, I've never seen anything this terrifying," Kian cries from a cloud of tear gas before shouting, "Death to the dictator!" once again. The young man has been lucky today. He has managed to outwit the Basiji militiamen who were lying in wait in the next alley along. Unfortunately, this is not the case for many of his fellow protesters.

"*Khodaya*. They've all been arrested. *Khodaya*, what should I do?"

Directly in front of him, a Robocop charges his motorbike toward the demonstrators on foot. This time, however, they are too big in number for him, and with a little difficulty and a few scrapes, they manage to knock him from his vehicle. Furious, they run toward the bike and set it alight before turning on its owner. While several young people approach him threateningly, others block the way, protecting their attacker, even tending to his wounds.

"Brother, why are you attacking the people?" they ask. "You should support us, we beg you." They then address the crowd. "We won't fix anything with violence. This is the best way to show him who we really are."

A tear rolls down the guitarist's cheek. "It's incredible. Only in Iran . . ."

A group of the police officer's colleagues arrive on the scene and do not share this philosophy of kindness. Without a hint of mercy, they trigger their water cannons, sending several protesters literally flying through the air. One young woman approaches them.

"Don't you have any family? Are you not Iranians like us? How can you be capable of such cruelty?"

In response, one officer pins the girl up against a wall and strikes her half a dozen times with his billy club. His victim covers her face with her hands and waits for the ordeal to be over. It finally ends as another group of protesters intervene by throwing stones, finally overwhelming her attacker.

"Bunch of bi-namous [someone who has neither mother nor sister], I would shit on your parents' souls," they chant. Fortunately, a cell phone has captured the entire scene.

"Today, the whole world will see the true face of this regime," Kian concludes. But the day is not over yet for our heroes. Four officers on motorbikes, armed with MP5 machine guns, also witnessed this scene and charge in their direction in an attempt to scare them off. The protesters manage to take cover in an adjacent alley where a mosque imam opens the door to them.

Despite the number of wounded, not a single ambulance is at the scene to take care of the protesters. Some are treated on the spot whereas others are carted off by the militiamen who also go to great pains to clear the street of any corpses before night falls. A few of the luckier ones are taken into neighboring homes while others are evacuated in the cars of friends they have made that very morning. This is the case for Kian, who transports a young seventeen-year-old who was clipped in the thigh with a bullet.

"It hurts, I'm dying . . ." the boy whimpers.

"Don't worry, my friend," the guitarist smiles. "You have the best wound there is. You'll be able to tell your kids all about how you got injured during your revolution."

"Yeah, that's true, but it hurts . . ." he continues to whine.

Kian decides to drive him to an uncle of his, a doctor, deeming that to take the boy to one of the city's many hospitals would be too dangerous. "The security forces will arrest any injured person that walks into those places," Kian explains.

Back at Hamid's office supply company, insults are flying as Arya pulls at the few hairs left on his head, struggling to be patient with the connection speeds.

"Fuck . . . Isla . . . Repu . . ." He is losing his temper, but he does not let this discourage him. He has already managed to post a dozen or so videos since this morning, and this time they are far different from those he had on Monday.

"Young people rolling on the ground, war scenes, beaten women, shots into the crowd . . ."

He is currently uploading the most recent clip, by far the most shocking to date, which has only just made it into his hands. Arya cannot hold back his tears as he describes the scene.

"A young female protester was shot in the middle of the street by a sniper. She is in agony and bleeds to death in a matter of seconds." The journalist dries his tears and sends the video off to over a hundred recipients.

"This scene is just like those I've heard about from my father, from the 1979 revolution. There too, a peaceful demonstrator was savagely killed by the Shah's police. I fear that we have reached the point of no return." He shakes his head.

Sources from inside the capital city's hospitals put today's death toll at "between thirty and forty protesters." Other reports claim that it is closer to one hundred and fifty.

"I'd say, trust the second figure," Arya warns.

Outside the capital, clashes also erupted in Shiraz, Rasht, Tabriz, and Isfahan.

Tehran's chief of police, General Ahmad-Reza Radan, announces that four hundred police officers have been injured over the past week and that there have been complaints from ten thousand people, sick of the "interruptions to their daily lives." These people, apparently, have called on the police to "act firmly."

16

"A RAY OF SUNSHINE" is the phrase used over and over by people talking about Neda. At twenty-six years old, this young Iranian woman's thirst for life and hope are impressive. She comes from a family of three children, her father a civil servant and her mother a housewife, and spends her days in Tehran Pars, a neighborhood in the capital's east.

Life has not always been kind to this young woman. Profoundly religious, she studied Theology and Islamic Philosophy at Azad University in Tehran, but she was not far into the first year of her studies when she realized that she did not recognize her God in the teachings of the school. After much consideration, she made the painful decision to leave the university.

Neda married young, but was soon divorced. A single woman once more, she began to look for work, but at each interview she was mocked and ridiculed as soon as her situation in life became known. In Iran, it is widely believed that for a woman to be divorced, there must be something wrong with her. And so, reluctantly, she decides to stay at home with her mother, where she quickly discovers that she is not cut out for the stay-at-home-woman role so carefully shaped for her by the regime. For while the Islamic Republic does what it can to demoralize its youth, all that its restrictions really succeed in doing is increasing their sensibilities. This is why so many of them find refuge in art, and Neda is no exception to this rule. Her passion is music, mostly Persian pop, a genre officially banned by the regime but widely available through satellite stations and the Internet.

On top of this, the young woman is learning to play the piano and, worst of all from the regime's perspective, is also secretly taking singing lessons. Her teacher will happily tell anyone who asks that his student's voice is nothing if not "divine." A risky business, given that for thirty years, women in Iran have not been authorized to so much as raise their voices, but as you are probably beginning to realize, there are many things that go on in the basements of the Iranian capital.

Neda's passion for art extends beyond the confines of music. Like many of her peers, she is more interested in self-cultivation than mindless television-watching; the young woman takes a great interest in literature, notably the Iranian poet Rumi and the American Robert Frost. Also, just because she has to be fully covered outside of the house, it does not necessarily follow that she neglects her body, and Neda spends hours working her abs and thigh muscles at the gym and doing lengths at the local women's swimming pool.

As the years have gone by, however, satellite television and the Internet have not been enough to satisfy her desires to discover the world, and so it is that the few savings she has are used exclusively to finance her travels. An Iranian passport is not what it once was under the Shah, and even less so since Ahmadinejad's arrival in office. Only those with enough money in the bank can convince tour operators to organize group trips abroad, allowing them to discover other countries within the region. The three top destinations are Dubai, Thailand, and Turkey, the latter holding a particular appeal for Iran's younger generation. It is one of the few countries that they may visit without a visa, and here, Neda discovers the Iran of which she has always dreamed. A Muslim country but secular state, this is the Iran her parents promised to offer her when they took part in the revolution thirty years ago. In her vacation photos, Neda can be seen stretched out in the Antalya waters, her headscarf safely packed away in her suitcase.

All of this is enough to make up her mind: she wants to be a tour guide. On returning to Tehran, driven by the profound desire to open her peers' eyes to the beauty of the overseas world, she enrolls in private tourism classes and even begins to study Turkish. It was during one of these group trips to Turkey, two months previously, that she met Caspian, a thirty-eight-year-old photographer, also divorced. Despite the short nature of their fleeting holiday romance, deep emotions have taken hold of the two lovers, and they have decided to get engaged, buying tickets to return to Istanbul together at the end of

June. In the meantime, however, events back home in Iran will alter their lives and their country forever.

Neda has never been particularly interested in politics, has never considered herself a member of any political party, and is one of the many people disappointed in the Islamic Republic. Throughout her entire life, any elections that have taken place have offered only the choice between a few carefully selected candidates. Her dreams of reform under President Khatami had quickly dissolved, and as a result, neither the dire consequences of the incumbent President Ahmadinejad's first term nor the potential hope offered by the reformist Mousavi had been enough to drive her to the ballot box this time around. Two weeks before the election, however, something changed. The Green Movement was born and the streets overcome with a carnival atmosphere. The excitement was contagious and could not possibly pass Neda by. While she was certainly not a Mousavi supporter, given that he was not a liberal candidate, she did love his supporters.

Outraged, like many of her fellow Iranians, by the unfair outcome of the election and the resulting insult paid to millions of her own people, she joined the protests from the start, accompanied by her mother or her fiancé. She wished to stand up for her freedom and for that of her people. Caspian knew from the start that this was a brave and strong woman, but he could not help worrying about her. To his concerns, she would simply reply, "Don't worry, Caspian, this is my destiny. We all have a responsibility to act in these current circumstances. If we had a child, I would carry him to the protests on my back." It was on that day that her future husband realized that he could never prevent her from taking part.

On June 19, everything changed. The supreme leader stood up alongside Ahmadinejad once and for all, authorizing the forces to quell the demonstrations, with blood if necessary. But like Azadeh, Kian, and Omid, Neda paid no heed to his threats and returned to the streets the very next day. Bombarded with phone calls from her best friends, begging her not to risk her life, she replies, "Quit worrying. It's just one bullet, and it's over anyway."

On Saturday, dressed in jeans, tennis shoes, T-shirt, and black baseball cap, Neda enters Kargar Street with her music teacher and heads towards Niloufar Square to join the thousands of protesters gathered there. She calls her mother several times, telling her about the many clashes between police and demonstrators. Tear gas hurtles toward the crowds, and Neda steps into a clinic to rest her eyes for a while. Twenty minutes later, she calls her mother one last time to reassure her that she has decided to turn back and heads toward her car, parked a little farther down. "She wasn't more than twenty-six steps away from her car," her mother later recounts. Twenty-six: also Neda's age.

At six thirty, as he is about to reach his student's car, Hamid Najafi, Neda's music teacher and close friend, hears the deafening sound of a gunshot. Spinning around, he sees Neda fall backward, staggering as she looks down at her upper body, a large stain spreading across her T-shirt. She has taken a bullet right in the middle of her chest. The young woman collapses to the ground.

"I'm burning. I'm burning . . ." she murmurs to her teacher.

"Neda, don't be afraid," he replies. "Don't be afraid. Please, whatever you do, don't be afraid . . ."

Neda turns her head to the right and looks directly at a protester who is capturing the horrific scene on his cell phone. Her eyes are a shining white, the color of innocence. "The eyes of death," her mother will later say.

At that moment, blood pours from her nose, her mouth, and her eyes. "Press down on it . . . Press down on it!" screams a young man who has just arrived at her side. Hamid Najafi and Arash Hamid, the doctor who by coincidence is also present at the scene, do everything they can to stop the hemorrhage. Neda's headscarf slips back into a pool of blood as the teacher's cries of "Don't be afraid" escalate.

Piercing screams of "Vay [Oh my God]!" from men as well as women, rebound around the street.

"You asshole!" one protester cries toward the man who fired the shot. The young woman's entire face is now covered with blood.

"Neda, don't go," another man cries as he crouches at her side. "Don't go . . . Don't go." He tries to open the victim's mouth with his fingers, but the effort is in vain. "Open your mouth . . ."

Neda bleeds to death in a matter of seconds and is dragged into the car, which will drive her to Tehran's Shariati hospital.

You may feel that you have seen this scene somewhere before because, of course, you have. You know Neda, as everybody knows Neda. This name, which in Persian means "voice," "call," and "divine message," has made it around the world, thanks to the protester who filmed the scene on his cell phone. With this clip, he was able to reveal the barbaric actions of this regime to the rest of the world and to put a name and a face to all victims of Iran's repression. Thanks to this, Neda has now earned the international nickname, "the voice of Iran."

In the instants that follow this scene, the crowd rushes toward a Basiji militiaman a few yards away. "I didn't mean to kill her, I didn't mean to kill her," he repeats through his tears.

"Don't hurt him. We're not murderers like them," the protesters cry as they take his weapon, strip him of his T-shirt, and confiscate his Basiji identity card before letting him escape, knowing full well that to hand him over to the police would be completely pointless. This card will later be published on the Internet. The perpetrator's name is Reza Kargar Javid, and he has still not been brought to justice by the Iranian legal system despite the fact that on June 29, Mahmoud Ahmadinejad labeled Neda's death "suspicious" and ordered a judicial inquiry into its circumstances.

Shiite Muslim identity has long been defined in the cult of martyrdom, and realizing the extent to which the death of a young Iranian woman under these circumstances would affect the population, the country's authorities did everything within their power to quash the affair. Neda's body was confiscated and her mother was not allowed to see it until immediately before the burial. She was given permission to inter her daughter, but only in a rudimentary grave in the section of the Behesht Zahra (Zahra's heaven) cemetery reserved for protesters. The organization of any ceremony in memory of her daughter was strictly forbidden, and none of the surrounding restaurants, lounges, or mosques was authorized to receive the party. As a final insult, Neda's family was not even permitted to display black banners on their front door, as custom dictates.

While all of this was going on, police officials appeared on television to blame her death on terrorist elements, insisting that government forces were not even equipped with firearms. They went on to suggest that Neda may have been on a suicide mission, bringing on her own death in order to destabilize the state. Outraged by these statements, Neda's fiancé Caspian multiplied his interviews on foreign news stations in order to spread the truth to a wider audience. He was consequently imprisoned for two months in the sinister political prison of Evin where he was forced to retract his statements and to flee the country. Arash Hejazi, the doctor who tried to save Neda, is now living in exile in the United Kingdom. According to Mohammad Javad Larijani, head of Iran's Council for Human Rights, "He is responsible for this criminal act, and the British government refuses to extradite him."

The day following Neda's death, her music teacher Hamid Panahi announced that "she was someone who was full of joy . . . She was a ray of sunshine, and I am devastated. I had great hope for this woman." A few days later, however, he is dragged in front of the television cameras to deny everything he previously claimed to have seen.

Neda's grave has now become a pilgrimage site for members of the opposition movement, but even in death, she is not safe from the Islamic Republic's bullets. One morning, her mother had to suffer the sight of her daughter's gravestone peppered with bullet holes.

17

SOHRAB ARABI IS THOUGHT OF as his family's big hope. Nineteen years old, this youngest brother of three already looks set for a bright future. For a year now he has been sequestered in his room at home, cramming for the notoriously difficult national university entrance examination. The higher he ranks, the more prestigious the establishment to which he will be assigned, and fully aware that attendance at one of the country's great universities is a ticket to a visa for overseas, Sohrab is determined not to fail. So far, the young man's life has not exactly been a bed of roses, and his extreme sensitivity is tangled up with deep feelings of melancholy. It was he who nursed his father during his long deterioration toward death, which finally came for him just two years ago.

Sohrab was quick to find his place within the Green Movement, keen to fight for his right to think freely and live in peace and tranquility. He knows full well that his ideals are in direct contrast to those of Ahmadinejad, and a few days before the start of voting, he is photographed wearing a green scarf, green headband, and green ribbon around his wrist, accompanied by his mother, Parvin Fahimi. The two have been closer than ever since his father's death. Parvin Fahimi, a staunch activist, is a member of the collective *Mothers for Peace*, who gather, often without authorization, to protest violence, war, and the execution of minors. These are the same mothers who sent an open letter to the authorities, condemning the nuclear program, and the same women who protested the war in Gaza in December 2008.

Both outraged by this year's election results, Sohrab and his mother took to the streets together on June 15, 2009, to protest in silence, much like our friend Azadeh. On this day, the crowds are enormous—over three million protesters are present—and it is not uncommon to see people who have lost track of those they came with, as is the case for Sohrab and Parvin. With cell phone networks down, Parvin has no way to contact her son and decides to go home to see if he has returned. On seeing that he has not, she heads off again in the direction of Azadi Square, now accompanied by the rest of the family.

"The atmosphere was just awful," she remembers. "The air was thick with tear gas; it was like a battlefield. My breathing hasn't been the same since." Parvin is forced to turn back, but she is anxious. "My son didn't have his identity card on him, just a small amount of cash which he planned to use to pay his examination fees, which were coming up soon."

That night quickly turned into a long, painful ordeal as the authorities announced the deaths of seven protesters. Of the seven victims, only five had been identified, and Sohrab was not among them. It was now just a question of the other two, although it sounded as though they were much older than Sohrab. Parvin can breathe easily again, sure that her son is still alive.

Thinking that he may have been wounded, Parvin, armed with a photo of her child, begins to do the rounds of the city's hospitals. No success here either, and she is again relieved. Her son must be OK. She is no longer in any doubt that he must have been arrested, and so she heads off on a tour of the city's police stations, courts, and prisons, in particular Evin Prison, where hundreds of protesters have been incarcerated. As prisoners are released, she runs toward them, brandishing Sohrab's photo to ask if anyone has seen her boy.

"Never seen him" is the answer each and every time.

She now questions one of the prison guards, a man with a thick beard. "I will call you, ma'am. This is almost the last of them," he says sternly.

She takes some comfort from the other families who have also lined up outside Evin, looking for their own lost loved ones. This anxiety-ridden, fruitless search will go on for twenty-six days of seemingly interminable torture until finally, on July 11, once the tenth anniversary of the 1999 student revolt has passed, it seems that it may be over. Parvin receives a call from the Revolutionary Court, asking her to come immediately to the Shapour police station. She will finally have some news of her son and has already anticipated having to pay a hefty sum in order to assure his swift release.

On arrival she is given a sheet of head shots to look over. Reminiscent of a yearbook photo page, there is one major difference: the people featured on this sheet of paper are dead. There are over sixty of them, each with a printed number below the body, none of them over thirty, and each a victim of the postelection protests. An interesting fact when you consider that the authorities put the official death toll at a mere twenty. Photo number twelve shows the lifeless body of a young man, laid out in a bathtub to be washed, still smiling through his soft teenager's beard, his left arm extended. It is Sohrab. The authorities inform his mother that her son was shot through the heart on June 15 as he protested. The body, however, was not registered at the morgue until June 19, four days later. The police claim that the reason it took so long to announce the death was that the boy did not have his identity card on him and was therefore difficult to identify. A few Iranian media sources overseas will later claim that Sohrab was tortured to death at Evin Prison, especially after the boy's aunt, Farahnaz Mohamadi, reveals that a second bullet wound could be seen below the back of his neck.

Two days later, on July 13, Sohrab is buried in Behesht Zahra cemetery, the same site where Neda's body was laid to rest. The ceremony is brief, conducted under the watchful eyes of security agents who allow Parvin to say but a few words, the closest thing she will get to a memorial for her son. Never mind that Shiite Muslim tradition—which the Iranian regime claims to uphold—has it that the deceased should be commemorated on the third, seventh, and fortieth day following the burial. On top of this, the authorities have ordered complete silence, threatening that any protest will lead to arrests and serious consequences for the Arabi family. Despite this, around five hundred people, among them many other mothers—anonymous for the most part—showed up to today's ceremony.

"*Allahu Akbar*," they chant angrily, many with hands raised high. They carry roses, cell phones, or simply display their V for victory finger signs.

"What they did to you, no other animal would ever do to one of his kind," one man says after reading a poem in Sohrab's honor.

Though she has shown great composure thus far, Parvin literally throws herself onto the shroud which covers her son's body, screaming, "I want to see him, I want to see him."

According to a well-known Iranian human rights activist, who prefers to remain nameless, "The bodies of those killed during the protests, or following prison torture and beatings, are only given to the family if they promise not to go to the media about their child's case. . . . The actual number of deaths is probably in the hundreds." He adds, "But it is impossible to say exactly how many, given that many families are scared into silence."

Once her son is buried, however, Parvin will not let herself be intimidated. Quite the opposite, in fact. "I will not keep quiet," *Sohrab's mother*, as she is now universally known, confirms.

"How could they kill my child and the children of others?" she continues. "Did they deserve to die just because they were protesting and asking for their vote back? . . . Our Sohrab is not dead, but the government certainly is."

Parvin also announced that she and her family would make her son's death into a rallying cry for the opposition, regardless of the consequences. As promised, every Saturday, *Mothers for Peace* and their supporters gather at Tehran's Laleh park, dressed in black. Parvin has succeeded, even excelled, in making Sohrab, like Neda before him, into an icon for the opposition to such an extent that protesters carry photos of the boy at every demonstration and that even Mir-Hossein Mousavi and his wife Zahra Rahnavard have paid a personal visit to his mother. The boy's killers, however, remain at large. A number of human rights organizations have called for an independent inquiry into Sohrab's death, but to no avail. The teenager should have had his university entrance exam at the beginning of July. His mother, at least, was able to discover what happened to her child and was given the opportunity to bury him. Over a month later, hundreds of other families are still without news of their loved ones, and there are still a great number of unclaimed orphans whose faces are among the Islamic Republic's head shots.

Sohrab Arabi quickly became a symbol for the victims of governmental repression, and a poem summarizing his mother's difficult journey was written in his honor.

> How quickly you grew up, Sohrab,
> During the twenty-six days that your mother looked
>   for you from door to door,
> How many years did you gain?
> The medical examiners saw fit at nineteen,
> To place you in the photo album of those at
>   twenty-five,
> You took a bullet on June 15,
> Open your eyes,
> Your mother cannot put down your photo.

18

"ALL THESE DEMONSTRATORS are just a bunch of hoodlums." This is Reza's opinion on the events that have hit his country over the last two weeks, a surprising view considering that he himself voted for the reformist Mousavi. "I feel let down by what has happened," he admits, "and we must prepare for hard days ahead. But we also have to sit and think seriously for a minute. How could he possibly fabricate thirteen million votes?"

Reza did not believe the rumors four years ago either, when a little-known candidate by the name of Ahmadinejad was accused of cheating his way to the second round. "These young people believed that things were going to change, and I understand that they're disappointed," he continues. "But to go from being disappointed to plunging the country into a bloody war is a big leap."

Needless to say, he has not participated in any of the protests that continue to rock the country. "I don't have the time to waste on these silly games. I have a job, something which these students and spoiled rich kids don't know anything about. Tell me, if I join arms with them, who is going to feed my family?"

The taxi driver has got it wrong. Many of the protests, such as the June 16 rally in Toopkhaneh Square, have been taking place in the south of the capital, in neighborhoods far more working-class than the affluent areas of the north. "No one there was actually from the south," he refutes this argument, although given that he has not been down there once himself, he has no proof of this.

Today, Reza is furious, although his reasons are not the same as those of his peers. In order to control the protesters, the police have blocked off the capital's main roads, which in turn has forced thousands of Iranians into smaller adjacent roads, the result of which is complete traffic chaos.

"By taking to the streets, they are ruining my livelihood," he exclaims. His half day of work in the taxi has proven to be practically fruitless, a situation which will be reflected this evening in the number of pieces of meat in his mother's *ghormeh sabzi*. On top of this, the window of his computer store was smashed the day before yesterday by the special security forces. Reza knows exactly who to blame for all of this.

"It's all Mousavi's fault. Why does he insist on winding up the crowds? I know it was the police that broke it, but the protesters are just provoking them. And Mousavi was the one who called them into the street in the first place."

What does he have to say about the tens, if not hundreds, of deaths? About the horrific images which have been plastered all over foreign Persian-language television stations?

"Listen, the police are there to protect us. They're not crazy. They find themselves faced with a minority group of rioters, hooligans who don't give a damn about the election. I mean, these people are trying to overthrow the regime."

Perhaps Reza somehow missed the video of Neda's last agonizing moments?

"Of course I saw it. Who didn't? It's awful, but I'm just saying that we don't have all of the details. And I'll bet you that there have not been as many deaths as they are reporting overseas," he says, echoing the authorities' position, which has been playing on loop on state television.

This position is not shared by Reza's mother and sisters, firm believers in the Islamic Republic, who nonetheless cry their eyes out each night as they prepare dinner in front of the television.

"*Khodaya*. What have these children done to deserve such treatment?" they wail.

"They're just overemotional and have nothing better to do than sit in front of the television all day," Reza smiles. Arriving back home, however, the smile fades, and the young man loses his temper once more, although this has nothing to do with the fact that his dinner is not yet ready.

"It's a real pain in the ass, the way they're cutting the Internet and phone networks. I can't send any business emails or even call my clients." Of course what he is really missing is his access to worldsex.com and the evening phone calls he usually makes to his many love interests.

Unlike Reza, many of the neighborhood's inhabitants voted for Ahmadinejad, but after a week of shocking events and signs of ferocious repression they find hard to believe, they are slowly starting to drift over to the opposition camp despite the presidential traveler's checks they recently received.

"How dare he kill our children like this in broad daylight?" cries Reza's neighbor Mahvash, a mother herself. "And how can the supreme leader offer him his support?"

"Pardon me, ma'am," Reza butts in, "but you have to try and remember our leader's words. The election broke all previous participation records, and each candidate is part of this regime. Some are trying to exploit that today, saying that the election was a regime defeat. You mustn't fall into their trap."

"*Khafeh sho, Reza* [literally, 'go suffocate yourself,' or 'shut up']. Go down there tomorrow and take a walk around Toopkhaneh Square, you'll see who's attacking who."

"Ma'am, there have never been debates like this before in Iran. It's a sign that our country is finally moving forwards."

The conversation is over and the two neighbors step inside, still unconvinced by the other's argument.

Crashing at a friend's house for the night—a friend who, for obvious reasons, must remain nameless—Arya is beginning to get used to changing address every night. He has finally finished his uploads at Hamid's place and must concentrate now on saving his skin.

"My friends, my colleagues, everyone who participated in either Mir-Hossein Mousavi or Mehdi Karoubi's campaigns are slowly being arrested, one by one. They're accused of acting against national security interests and that could mean big trouble. *Khodaya*, I'm next on the list."

Two days ago, the journalist's parents, who live in the provinces, received a rather unfriendly visit from three officers on his trail. "Your son is collaborating with the enemy by fabricating reports to bring down the regime," they were told. "Either you tell us where he is, or you're coming with us."

Fortunately, or unfortunately depending on how you look at it, Arya's parents have no idea as to where he can be found. He has also disposed of his cell phone as well as his memory chip after a heads-up that the phone company Nokia-Siemens was providing the Islamic Republic with equipment to track his conversations and online discussions.

"Unfortunately, we've had to get used to Westerners betraying us like that," the student laughs. "And once they've got you on their radar, the Iranian intelligence services are worse than the Mossad."

Despite all of the threats, he wishes to share his thoughts on one particular subject, or rather on one particular kind of person. "Seventy percent of Iranians live in urban areas. Between 30 and 35 percent of them make up what we call the nation's middle class. These are rural inhabitants who decided, after the revolution, to move to the country's main cities where they now work as laborers, tradesmen, workers, and taxi drivers. While their lifestyle may be middle class, their culture is not. They are greatly lacking in awareness and cultural roots. I'm sorry to say it, but you could almost say they were idiots. Despite what they say, they don't understand a single thing about politics. One day they let their emotions get the better of them and they vote for Khatami. Four years later, they find themselves sucked in by propaganda and vote for Ahmadinejad in the second round. You show them the proof that there were enormous levels of fraud during the *first* round, and they still don't believe you. Now this time around, they get picked up and carried along by Mousavi's Green Movement.

"History has shown that the candidate chosen by these people always wins the presidential race and succeeds in keeping them happy for his first four-year term. The difference this year is that their candidate lost. This has finally led them to become aware of the extent of the fraud and of the abuses of power in the government, and they have taken to the streets, surrounded by students and intellectuals. I guess at least now we can say that they're a little less ignorant than they were before. They have come to see the democratic farce that this religion-based regime has been putting on and they're no longer willing to swallow everything they're told. The Islamic Republic has gone down in their estimation, has lost its legitimacy, and that is a very big deal. Next time there's an election, they won't go to vote because they know that there is no point. That's where we're at now, and it's huge."

Haunted by her words, Reza will finally take his neighbor Mahvash's advice. It is Sunday, June 28, and he has decided to take his car for a spin around Shariati Street, in front of the Qoba Mosque. Here, protesters are making the most of the opportunity afforded them by the anniversary of Ayatollah Beheshti's death—commemorated each year—to stage a rally. When you combine something useful with something enjoyable, the results are even greater, and so Reza is delighted to see an enormous line of people waiting at the taxi station on Reza-Abad Avenue, hoping to catch a ride to the event. Spotting the potential gold mine, he completes several round-trips at one thousand tomans ($1) per person instead of the usual five hundred (50¢), making up for his lack of wages over the last two weeks.

"That's daylight robbery, my child," the mother of one family cries.

"Long live Ahmadinejad," is his response, and the two burst out laughing.

Next, Reza lets in a group of six people: one in the passenger seat, one practically on top of the hand brake, and four in the backseat.

"Let's hope that all this isn't in vain," the woman smiles. "Because I for one am starting to get a sore butt." The group bursts into laughter.

A young teenager with gelled hair, pressed up against the back windscreen, suddenly asks, "Did you hear what Ahmadinejad just announced? Iran beat South Korea 4–0 in the qualifier and is headed for the 2010 World Cup. There's proof at the Ministry of Interior. And anyone that says otherwise will be considered to be starting a riot and treated accordingly." Again, the taxi fills with laughter.

Next up is a young woman, seated in the middle, thus far more preoccupied with her neighbor's wandering hands than anything else.

"What were Ahmadinejad's first words as he reached the end of his first term?" she jokes. "Well, I'm done, does anyone else need to use the toilet?" Reza is laughing so hard that tears roll down his cheeks.

This good cheer, however—a trademark of the Iranian people during tough times—is really a mask for deep sadness and troubling fear. With the exception of Reza, everyone currently crammed into the old Peykan has a loved one or acquaintance in jail. This is the case of the eldest woman, who has had no news of her nephew for over ten days.

"His mother is so distraught that she won't even leave the house. It is our duty to carry on the fight," she sighs. "For our sense of pride, for our people, for all the innocents who have been killed, and for our future. I hope you're on our side, my child," she says to the driver.

Evidently embarrassed, Reza mutters shyly, "Of course . . . of course . . ."

They arrive at their destination and pull in under the Seyed-Khandan Bridge, a stone's throw from the mosque. The passengers slip into their masks and tie ribbons around their wrists, looking preoccupied as their mother gives them her final blessing.

"May God protect you," she utters as a sign of encouragement before reminding them, "Just don't forget how many of us there are today."

They step out of the taxi and head toward the gathering, unsure of whether they will make it home at the end of the day. Moved by this scene, Reza decides that rather than heading straight off on another round-trip, he will take a quick drive around the edges of the demonstration.

A couple hundred feet along and his vehicle is forced to a standstill, surrounded on all sides by protesters. Instead of hitting the wheel in frustration, Reza takes a look around him. This is far from the group of soccer hooligans he had been led to imagine. What he is witnessing is thousands of Iranians of all shapes and sizes: many women, but also the elderly, the young, and people from the south, just like himself.

"*Allahu Akbar*" they chant in one voice, waving their V for victory finger signs in the air. The noise is deafening and gives Reza goose bumps.

"*Dameshoon garm.*" *The young* man is beside himself. "There you have it, the Iranian people . . ."

"Come join us," an elegant young woman of around his age extends her hand toward his open window. He could never have imagined such a scene, not even in his wildest dreams.

All of a sudden, a young man starts clambering up a wall on the other side to get the attention of the crowd. "Don't go up there, don't go up there!" a young female voice rings out. "For God's sake, get down, right now. Please, I beg you. You'll get shot . . ."

Shocked by the reaction, the young man climbs back down immediately, but a few minutes later, the dreaded moment arrives. As the crowd continues to protest peacefully, the special police forces and Basijis launch their attack. Dozens of officers pounce on those gathered, billy clubs and knives at the ready. Reza, who asked for none of this, is startled as in a matter of seconds his car window explodes under the pressure of a Robocop club.

"Stop, stop! I'm not one of them," he cries to no avail.

"Shut it, sucker," the officer replies. "Infidel, mercenary, fool . . ." he shouts as he takes out the windscreen once and for all. "Maybe that'll teach you to try and take down the regime."

Infidel? Mercenary? Reza has never been insulted like this in his life; he who for his entire existence has held Islam and the Islamic Republic in such high regard. The young man begins to feel uneasy.

Amidst the chaos, he suddenly catches sight of a woman in her forties who has been pushed aside by a heavy, bearded man and is now being thrown violently to the ground. Evidently injured in the leg, she struggles to get up as her attacker moves toward her again. Separated only by a manhole in the middle of the street, he takes out his billy club and serves up six swift lashes, some aimed directly at her head. Paralyzed with fear and covered in blood, the young woman cannot stop crying. Reza, witnessing the whole thing, steps out of his car.

"Hey, asshole, don't you have a mother of your own, or any sisters?" he screams. "How dare you attack our mothers like this!"

Hearing his words, the crowd suddenly becomes aware of the situation and rushes toward the militiaman, who in turn takes off as fast as he can. The taxi driver takes the victim in his arms and lays her down on the backseat of his car. The crowd parts to let them pass.

"Don't worry, you'll be fine. I'll take care of you. I'm taking you to the hospital."

"Thank you, my boy," she mutters, "and don't worry, we'll win in the end."

19

*A*T TWENTY-EIGHT YEARS OLD, Taraneh Mousavi is a stunning *dokhtar irooni* (Iranian woman). With a model's body, piercing green eyes, and thick black eyebrows, she wears her hair in a braid that hangs down from her green headscarf. It is her sharp fashion sense, picked up mostly from satellite television stations, which has led her to follow her chosen career path. Taraneh, whose name means "song" in Persian, is taking classes at Tehran's Beauty Institute. On June 28, she is on her way to school, at the intersection of Mirdamad and Shariati Boulevard. Parking her car in a side street, she looks up to see a group of hundreds of protesters gathered in front of the Qoba Mosque. Mir-Hossein Mousavi (who despite the name is in no way related to Taraneh) is giving a speech in memory of the protesters who have died as martyrs to the prodemocracy cause. Enticed by the spectacle, Taraneh calls a classmate and arranges to meet her in front of the mosque, to enjoy just a taste of the event before heading back to class. The young woman had already taken part in the preelection celebrations as well as in the silent demonstrations on June 15, 16, and 17.

Suddenly, from out of nowhere, a group of plainclothes Basijis launches an attack on the crowd. Despite being merely a bystander to this scene, the young woman's green coat and headscarf make her as much of a target as anyone else, and she is thrown into a truck along with a group of other young protesters. Taraneh will never make it to the meeting place she arranged with her friend.

The demonstrators are driven to a building near the Pasdaran neighborhood and interrogated one by one. Unfortunately for her, the young woman is wearing high heels and a considerable amount of makeup, and her interrogation takes much longer than that of the other people picked up at the same time. They will soon be released, but Taraneh's fate will be something altogether different. Realizing that she is not going to get out of this lightly, she asks for permission to call her parents to inform them of her whereabouts and to reassure them that their only child is safe.

After being released, one of the detainees will reveal, "We were put under both psychological and physical pressure by antiriot police officers and plainclothes Basijis. Taraneh was with us and wouldn't stop crying, trying to convince the militiamen that she was just there for her class. She's very beautiful, very tall and stylish, and her interrogation was by far the longest. We were freed that same night, but the Basijis kept Taraneh behind. They wouldn't even let her call her mother."

Several days later, the girl's mother and father locate their daughter's car, still parked in the same side street. The car is empty. After two painful weeks, they finally receive some news. An anonymous caller, in all likelihood one of their daughter's attackers, informs them over the phone that Taraneh has been admitted to Imam Khomeini Hospital in northwest Tehran, to be treated for "tear wounds to her vagina and anus," the results of an "unfortunate accident." He adds that their daughter tried to hang herself with a saline tube because of her "moral deficiency" and that this was "in no way related to the Qoba Mosque protest rally."

Moral deficiency, in the Islamic Republic, means that Taraneh had "consented" to sexual relations outside of marriage, the implication being that upon realizing that she would be seen as nothing but a prostitute, she was unable to bear the shame and decided to take her own life. Taraneh's mother replies that a number of witnesses have reported that her daughter had been arrested outside the Qoba Mosque and taken to a police station, and that therefore her death had everything to do with the protest rally.

The family rushes to the hospital as instructed, but the staff there claim not to have admitted any woman fitting her description. Just a moment later, however, one member of the hospital staff informs them that what he did see was "several *hezbolahi* [bearded] men" who had brought in a young girl with braided hair, in a comatose state, and that they had then taken her away to an undisclosed location. Taraneh's father, an older man with a history of heart problems, has to be hospitalized at this point.

On July 14, the couple receives yet another anonymous phone call, this time asking them to come and claim the body of their only daughter, which has been found, completely burned, in the desert between the cities of Qazvin and Karaj. The authorities, of course, go to great lengths to underscore to her parents that any media attention surrounding this incident would not come without severe reprisal. On top of that, rape and extramarital sexual relations are entirely taboo subjects in Iran, where society continues to be firmly anchored to its traditions. Rape victims and their families, in contrast to the relatives of murdered protesters, tend to be shunned by society and, more often than not, choose not to pursue the perpetrators.

This time the Islamic Republic is again victorious. Taraneh's parents do not speak out. Her friends, on the other hand, decide to step in and take the matter into their own hands. Taraneh's tragic fate causes such a stir, particularly on the Internet, that Mehdi Karoubi—the other reformist presidential candidate—will take her case to the authorities and create a parliamentary inquiry commission to deal with the rape of arrested protesters, beginning with this young woman's case. The case then travels across the globe to the U.S. Senate floor, where Michigan Republican Senator Thaddeus McCotter will make a speech alongside a blown-up portrait of the beautiful young woman to publicize the incident.

Directing his words toward the leaders of the Islamic Republic, he states, "Your referendum has been held and you have failed your test. Taraneh and Neda condemn you as the despicable killers of women. You have no legitimacy either in the eyes of the Iranian people or in the eyes of the civilized world. You are doomed by your own hands, and it is but a matter of time until your regime collapses and the Iranian people breathe free."

This causes such a stir that the Islamic Republic will later respond through the bias of their own state television. They will concoct a report in which a registry office employee will announce that there are only three Taraneh Mousavis on file: one aged twenty-five and currently living in Paris, a second aged forty and no longer resident in Iran, and a third aged only two years old. Not satisfied with that, state journalists go on to publicly show the now-famous photograph of Taraneh to another Iranian family. According to them, this is a picture of their forty-year-old daughter, now resident in Canada, who has not stepped foot inside the Islamic Republic for over a year.

"The announcement just made us laugh," they explain in reference to Taraneh Mousavi's death. "We thought that someone was playing a practical joke on us." The journalist even goes so far as to ask the family to call their beloved Taraneh in Canada, in the middle of the night.

"Hello, Taraneh? Listen, there are a bunch of Internet sites that have published your photo, saying that you've been . . . burned," her sister sniggers.

As if that were not enough, the mother suddenly flies into a rage. "I had spoken to my daughter on the phone and so I wasn't worried. But I wouldn't be surprised if it had caused others a great deal of pain and shock, perhaps even brought on heart attacks. I beg the government to please ensure that this kind of thing never happens again."

In their haste to act as news vigilantes, however, a number of substantial mistakes were made by the government. One simple Google search will reveal that another Taraneh Mousavi lives in Gorgan and a second, a sixteen-year-old musician with the band Orkideh, is also still resident in Iran. In fact, there are over one hundred and sixty Taraneh Mousavis throughout the country. But the most ridiculous errors are yet to come. The person described as a registry office employee was none other than General Ahmad Rouzbahani, head of the Iranian Moral Security Police. This piece of information was revealed by Persian-language satellite station Voice of America.

Mehdi Karoubi, now one of the leaders of the opposition, described this Iranian state television program as a "government conspiracy" in a letter, also stating that "a number of officials from the security and military forces, on learning of the existence of a Taraneh Mousavi living overseas, rushed to pay a visit to her husband's family in Tehran.

They asked him, for the good of the regime and as an important stage of the fight against Western media, to join forces with them and refute the death of Taraneh Mousavi. At the end of this 'interview' the family asked the officials what had really happened to the Taraneh Mousavi in question and were told that it was none of their concern."

Again, according to Mehdi Karoubi, "The brother of this Canadian Taraneh Mousavi's husband did all that he could to prevent the interview from taking place, but just a few minutes later, the officials went to meet Taraneh's parents themselves, and there they got what they were after."

The final big mistake is revealed as Voice of America shows that the photograph used in the Iranian report—the very same one that was shown to the family of the Taraneh living in Canada—displays absolutely no likeness whatsoever to the Taraneh Mousavi who was raped and burned. It is clearly not the same person. This inconsistency is also raised in Mehdi Karoubi's letter, as he states, "The mother and sister felt so guilty that they had gone along with this story, that they then wished to reestablish the truth. In the end, however, after receiving a number of threats, they went back on their decision."

Unfortunately for the many Iranian victims and their families, this sophisticated fictional report is by no means the first of its kind.

The revelation of the atrocious murders that are to come will shake Iran's younger generation to the core. But while they will be greatly affected, they will by no means be defeated. Kian, Sassan, and Koushyar, who have not picked up their instruments for over a month now, are testaments to this as they decide to reunite. The haunting chords of Kian's acoustic guitar reverberate around Niavaran's basements. The young man closes his eyes, from which floods of tears now fall. His two partners, now his brothers-in-arms, are in a similar state of distress as Kian and his bandmates sing for the youth of their country.

20

"ALLAHU AKBAR," a soft, female voice travels through the Tehran night, mingling with the sounds of the city's leaves, which rustle in the evening breeze. Today has seen new protests in the capital and with them, a considerable number of fatalities.

"*Allahu Akbar*," a deeper voice repeats, a little farther down from the first, shortly followed by a shriller version of the same phrase. Then come two female voices, one on top of the other, awkwardly passing along the message.

"*Allahu Akbar*." The snowball effect has kicked in, and before long, tens, and soon hundreds, of Iranians are roaring, "God is great" into the half-light of the night sky. It is 10:30 p.m, and in keeping with her new nightly ritual, Mandana has woken up her daughter to join her on the roof to chant the famous slogan. To help keep the girl's strength up, she has prepared some tea and a bowl of pistachios.

"*Allahu Akbar*," the young woman calls out shyly, quickly followed by the neighbors on the second floor, and then the third.

"How's it going, Azi?" her neighbor Mahmoud enquires, standing below in his undershirt and slippers. "What's up? How's your family?"

Over the last ten days, the likelihood of being shot down at one of the city's many protest rallies has become progressively higher, and the time has come to find other ways to get the message out there.

"*Allahu Ak . . .*," Mandana cries hoarsely before collapsing in a coughing fit. Her neighbors are bent double in laughter, amused at the spectacle of this mother having the time of her life out there this evening. "How time flies, I remember it like it was yesterday," she recounts. "My family made me shout this slogan, first at the Shah, and later at our Iraqi enemies. It was Khomeini who asked us to do it back then, and here it is today, being turned around and used against the mullahs."

Her daughter is just as excited. "The authorities say we can't demonstrate? Let's see how they're going to make us keep quiet now," she smiles in determination. From their rooftops, their balconies, or their windows, they hope to haunt their ayatollahs right through the night, and with God as their weapon of choice, this insomnia attack could last for a long, long time. These ingenious tactics allow the Iranian people to continue their protests and fight back from the safety of their homes. "No one in the Islamic Republic is going to arrest anybody for shouting 'God is great' along with thousands of their fellow people," Azadeh points out.

The added bonus is that this is a huge source of frustration for the powers that be. As state television announces that "troublemakers—allies of the West—are preventing people from sleeping," the authorities work to do everything in their power, and sometimes more, to put an end to this heresy. This evening, a dozen Basijis on motorbikes charge through the neighborhood, revving their 250cc engines as loudly as they can and finally stopping at the bottom of the building.

"*Khafeshin* [shut up]," they shout in their deep, gruff voices. "You just wait and see. We'll identify each and every one of you."

The only response to this threat is another round of "*Allahu Akbars*" reverberating all around. The militiamen spray graffiti on a few individual houses, kick down a couple of doors, and smash some windows, but there has to be a limit to what they can do faced with an entire nation peacefully expressing their anger in this way.

"*Ya Hossein* ['Long live Hossein,' Shiite imam worshipped by many in Iran]," Mandana cries at the top of her lungs, this time with a little more gusto.

"*Mir*-Hossein [Mousavi]," a chorus of female voices replies from a few buildings down. The neighbors hold each other tight, moved by what they are witnessing.

"That's my people for you, I love them so much," Azadeh cries. "This isn't just a protest, it's a kind of group therapy session for us. We can let it all out, vent our anger, pour out the contents of our hearts. We prove to ourselves and each other that we're not alone and this helps us to share energy and courage in preparation for what's next."

The chants also act as a kind of gauge, and the more bloody the day's events, the more the "*Allahu Akbars*" come in the form of moans and groans. "You can pretty much tell from the number of slogans you hear over the course of the night whether the rally the next day is going to go ahead or not," Azadeh explains. The most cries can be observed, for example, during the nights that follow speeches by the supreme leader.

As for the slogan rivalry that has developed, the couple opposite is proud to claim first prize tonight, much to the annoyance of their friends. Their "*Allahu Akbars*" are by far the loudest and most persistent of all, and Mandana struggles for breath to even keep up with them. Nobody could have guessed though, as they discover the following day, that the young married couple had in fact made a recording of themselves and were playing it back on their Dolby surround sound.

"Death to the dictator," Mahmoud, the neighbor, chants now, to the delight of the entire building's residents, who now take up that line instead.

As everyone knows, however, the morning after, a party is never easy, and when Azadeh gets up the next day, she finds that she has lost her voice. She is not the only one in her neighborhood, and she considers it a sign of a job well done. The Islamic Republic may well ban its citizens from demonstrating, and they may well kill them or lock them up, but they are forgetting one small detail. "There's just such a wealth of talent in Iran," Azadeh mutters, having a hard time, as always, waking up. "These days the big term is 'civil disobedience' and believe me, you can rely on the young people of Iran for that one."

The proof of this is in the countless green 1,000 tomans bills ($1), now annotated with the words "Death to the dictator" or "*Rayeh man kou*" (Where is my vote?). The authorities have even, on occasion, had to suffer the image of their beloved Imam Khomeini, founder of the Islamic Republic, decked out with devil horns or, worse still, with blacked-out eyes.

"Bank bills are the best way to pass messages to our peers and to our leaders," Azadeh chuckles. Having first threatened to void all bills of this kind, the government has been forced to go back on its word because of the sheer numbers of them in circulation. As for ball-point pens and green felt-tips, all of the stores have run out. Another popular tactic is to fill green balloons with helium, but if you are not the kind of person who keeps a spare gas tank lying around the house, there are still a good many options.

"Every morning there's some kind of practical guide in your mail-box about how to use kitchen salt or other household products to get what you need," Azadeh shouts in excitement. "That's the Iranian people for you, always making sure they have fun while at work . . . it's good for the soul."

Down in the street, it is fair to assume that any car honking its horn away to its heart's content, or blaring its beam headlights, is prob-ably part of the Green Movement. Tehran traffic being as heavy as it is, it is next to impossible that the person in question would ever get reported. Graffiti "hooligans" have also been running wild, decorating the walls of the city with antigovernment slogans in green spray paint, an act which before now would have been unthinkable in Iran.

As if these acts were not enough, three days before each scheduled speech by either the supreme leader or the president, strange emails start doing the rounds. Azadeh reads one out. "They're asking everyone to wait until exactly nine o'clock, when the news comes on, and then to turn on all of their appliances—irons, washing machines, lights—as high as they'll go, to see if we can overload the system and shut down power throughout the country. At the end of the email it asks you to pass the word on to all of your friends and, most importantly, to make sure that you erase the name of the person that sent it on to you, to help minimize the inevitable government crackdown."

This may sound implausible, but is in fact a tried and tested technique. During a live broadcast of the reelected president, the

139 GREEN RIBBONS AND TURBANS

country's electrical network went out for about a second, causing many of Tehran's neighborhoods to suffer complete power outages. "At that moment," Azadeh smiles, "every Internet user in the country understood that they had won."

To combat this sneaky sabotage attempt, the authorities find themselves forced, for these important periods of time, to shut down machinery known to consume high levels of electricity. "I bet you can't find one single elevator operating between seven and ten in the evening on those days," Azadeh laughs out loud.

This civil disobedience is not confined to these concrete, practical tactics. Rightfully blaming Iranian television for the huge role it played in spreading progovernment propaganda during the campaign, and also acknowledging that the large majority of commercials are for national companies, the population decides on another peaceful course of action: the boycott. All national, state-run brands are rejected, and this has a huge knock-on effect for advertisers, who in turn are becoming angry about the situation.

"In just one month," Azadeh is delighted to announce, "the number of bank, insurance, and car commercials shown at peak times, has plummeted. They want to kill us? Well then we'll kill their commercials."

And there is more. Upon learning that Nokia-Siemens had provided the Islamic Republic with phone tapping materials and Internet spy software, furious customers forced telephone stores in shopping centers around the capital to remove from display all products made by the Germano-Finnish company. Azadeh is one such client. "Several of my friends and I sold our Nokia phones, even though they get the best reception in the country," she boasts. "That's what we call *ergheh melli irooni* [Iranian national pride], the envy of the entire world." As a result, Nokia sales in Iran fell dramatically to half their previous rate.

Faced with their government's bullets, the people of Iran are fighting back with their minds. The most recent initiative: a boycott on all text-messaging, a practice which directly benefits Iranian telecom companies and really does not serve much purpose outside of telling a few jokes. The scheme is beginning to bear its fruits: Telecommunication Company of Iran recently announced that text message prices would double.

"Victory!" Azadeh rejoices.

21

"WE KNOW WHERE YOU'RE HIDING, my friend. You'd better pack your bags, we'll be right over . . ." This is the gist of the anonymous phone call that Arya has just received. Just one hour later and there is a knock at the door. It looks like the jig is up, and to put up a fight at this point seems futile.

"*Salam doostan* [Hi there, my friends]. It's been a while since I had the pleasure, I was just starting to miss you."

"Let's make up for lost time then." They laugh in his face. There are four of them, four tall men towering above him. The two sides stare each other down for what seems like an eternity then, in a flash, the agents jump on Arya and his friend.

"Leave him out of this, he has no connection to me," the journalist protests in vain.

"It's our turn to put him up for a while, that's all." This time they are not laughing.

Arya feels a sharp elbow hit his stomach followed by a round of violent punches. Barely conscious, his attackers take the opportunity to slip a blindfold over his eyes, an accessory he had better get used to quickly. Kicked now from all angles, the journalist passes out. Before losing consciousness, he remembers hearing the revving of a car engine, and then several hours later, he is awoken by a blinding light coming from the ceiling. Wherever he is, it smells of death. He is covered with dried bloodstains, laid out in a cell of miniscule proportions.

"It was probably about five feet by eight feet," he estimates. Directly in front of him is a large iron door, above and to the right of which is an air vent. Below the door there is a small gap. There is no hint of a doubt about it; this is an isolation cell, in all likelihood within the confines of Evin Prison. The student's future is beginning to look bleak.

He looks around and sees that his kidnappers have made a few small efforts to help him settle in. There is no mattress in the tiny space, but he does find a bottle of water and three sheets. "One sheet as a bed, the second as a blanket, the final one as a pillow," he explains. Perhaps the most generous of all is that they have provided a *mohr*, a sacred stone, so that he may pray.

Suddenly, he hears sandals on the concrete outside his cell. "Put on your blindfold," a deep voice orders.

"Please. Where am I?" the young man asks.

As a response, a powerful blow sends him reeling to the ground. "Next time you open your mouth, you're dead. Got it?"

Arya moves forward in complete darkness, guided vaguely by his jailor, until he finally reaches a much larger room. This he can tell by the echo of his host's voice, an imposing man whose voice is even rougher than the first. "Hello there, my friend," he begins. "I trust you had a good journey here? Now listen, you're not at your mother's house anymore, you know. You either work with me and you will be allowed to leave, or you refuse, and you've as good as signed your own death warrant. I'll crush you, my friend." As a welcome gift, the young man receives yet another round of punches before being thrown back into his cell.

Arya knows all too well what it would mean to "work with him." In the Islamic Republic, this too is equivalent to signing your own death warrant. By giving a forced confession, a prison sentence would be the best he could hope for; at worst he would be hanged. So far it has been a rough day; his body is covered with bruises, and he is simply exhausted. The light burns his eyes, quashing any hopes he may have had of a well-deserved rest. Wondering how to get rid of it, he looks around for a switch, but is not at all surprised to discover that the cell does not have one. He will just have to make do. Wrapped in his own arms, he bursts into tears. A second later, the sandals can be heard once again in the corridor.

"Put on your blindfold."

He finds himself in the same large room where he is pushed into a chair before the voice from earlier begins again. "You son of a bitch.

You're nothing, you know that? You are worth nothing. You're all alone. Did you really think that you could run your own little velvet revolution?" The interrogator cracks up laughing and strikes him across the face. "I'm going to ask you some questions. You will answer me quickly and accurately. If you don't, you know exactly what's going to happen. Got it?"

The questions are predictable. "What were you doing the day of the election? Who else attended the Mosharekat party[1] meetings?" Some, however, manage to take Arya by surprise. "Tell us how you organized the riots. How many members does your 'organization' have?" or even, "What were you plotting at the swimming pool all those Thursday nights?"

"The craziest thing is that they genuinely believe all that," Arya laughs now. To his great surprise, the interrogator is also quick to apologize.

"Sorry kid, I got a bit carried away. It's just that I'm at the end of my tether, and it's all thanks to you." It is clear that the man understands that this is no ordinary protester, and this makes Arya feel at least slightly respected.

"When he asked me for my email password," the journalist now reveals, "I knew exactly what was at risk, and I refused him. He just gave in, without saying a word."

"The interview is over," the agent announces, and not a word more. Arya is taken back to his cell.

"Evin's not so bad after all," the young man thinks to himself, this being his first visit to the notorious prison. The meals may not quite be up to Michelin standard, but at least he gets one three times a day. The biggest problem, however, is that it is impossible for him to close his eyes even for a second, and now, once again, he hears sandals heading in his direction. The interrogations will go on like this without a single break. When his interrogator starts to get tired and Arya glimpses his chance to rest, a colleague takes over, followed by another in turn. Just like in a hospital, things here operate on a rotation system. For five days and nights, Arya will not close his eyes. "You can barely stand up. You start to fall apart," he remembers.

On top of this, his torturer—sorry, his "interrogator"—has changed tactics again. "The questions are always the same. They repeat them over and over at an incredible pace, and if you don't give them the answer they're looking for, then they just ask exactly the same question again, as if you hadn't said anything at all. When they're done, they start at the beginning again. In the end, you just can't take it anymore."

Adding insult to injury, the day always ends on a mocking note. "Funny, you're writing much more slowly than yesterday. Come on, get a move on."

After the efforts exerted in the interrogation room, his cell starts to feel like paradise on earth, but it will quickly become an absolute hell. Each time he starts to doze off, Arya is woken for prayer, food, or another round of questioning. "You have no choice but to do what they say, unless you want another beating."

Another sneaky tactic is that his plate is only pushed halfway through the gap under the door, forcing him to get up himself to pull it through into his cell. When he finally does get a moment's peace, he finds that even that is not all it is cracked up to be. The inside of his cell is completely void of any distraction. There is no window or opening of any description, meaning that it is either constantly day or night, depending on what his captors decide. "There's nothing, absolutely nothing, to allow you to think. You go crazy. You have nothing left to cling to."

Then there is the physical torture. "You can't go to the bathroom when you want to. Often, the guard waits hours before allowing you to go, leaving you no choice but to do it right there. Things start to get bad, so you try your best to lose yourself in your dreams. But you know that at any second you'll be torn away from them again. You never get to fall into a deep sleep."

Then comes the real descent into hell. "They force your system to go into crisis mode. They take away your soul. You don't have a clue about what's going on around you. Your brain is starved of details and thoughts, and you're surrounded by an enormous void. You become so desperate for someone to talk to that it doesn't even matter who it is, and you end up simply dying to have a conversation with your guard."

Every time Arya tries to strike up a conversation, however, his guard replies with his fists. "So you find yourself actually longing to talk to your interrogator." So much so, that Arya cannot hide his pleasure when he finds himself once again in the man's presence.

"You missed me," he laughs at his prisoner, although he cannot possibly know just how much. The situation is about to take another about-turn as the interrogator becomes kinder, gentler than before.

He cocks his head. "Listen, kid, I'm really sorry, but outside it's all over. Your revolution has failed. Mousavi, Karoubi, and Khatami have all been arrested and have confessed to plotting against our leader. Nobody is wondering where you are; they've forgotten you even exist. Neither your family nor your friends nor anybody else has tried to find out what's happened to you. You're on your own. It's just you and you're going to die."

The young man's world comes crashing down around him. His newfound "God," the only person who has deigned to speak to him for days or even weeks—he can no longer remember—has just stamped out his final glimmer of hope.

"Listen, kid, I like you a lot," he goes on. "I'd like to do something for you. We must spare you from being hanged. You know, if you help me, then maybe I can pull a few strings and get you life instead."

Such generosity all of a sudden that Arya no longer knows what he should do. He forces himself to remember all of those political prisoners, including several of his friends who, in a similar situation, gave in in exchange for this unexpected offer of help. The confessions signed, their torturer congratulated them before informing them that in fact the statement they had signed was going to lead them straight to the gallows. That everything was over and their execution would now happen sooner than previously planned. "They keep their word on that one," the prisoner sighs.

Today, Arya turns the offer down. "At that point, you don't even care what happens to you. You feel strong, extremely strong," he explains. But the Islamic authorities are also feeling strong, and they will just have to try a different approach.

"Fine," the interrogator laughs. "You've made your choice. You can have it your way. Now let me see, here we have . . . a young woman.[2] This young woman is a student at the University of X. Yesterday she was spotted in X Street, visiting her Aunt X. The day before that, at five o'clock, she attended her music lesson as she does every week. Now, how would you like me to concoct a little criminal record for her?"

Arya begins to tremble. The torturer continues, "I'll fuck your sister. I'll bring her here and do it right in front on your eyes, you understand?" Arya shakes, knowing that these people are perfectly capable of such an atrocity.

"All they care about is climbing the ladder," he explains. "The more confessions a man manages to extract, the faster he advances up the hierarchy."

The torturer slips him a sheet of paper and a pen and begins to read the content aloud. "I confess to attempting to lead a revolution with the aim of overturning the Islamic Republic. I now believe the presidential elections to be entirely correct and see no reason to suspect any foul play. I beg forgiveness from the supreme leader.

"If you want to save your sister," he explains softly, "all you have to do is sign." Arya has not spent twenty-seven years under the Islamic Republic to give in now, and so he continues to refuse. This time, the interrogator will show his true colors, the proof of which can still be seen today, in the scars on the young man's body.

"It's still too difficult for me to talk about," he trembles. "All I can give you is a few hints: cigarettes, cutter, chains, bag, stick . . . at one point he even took my penis in his hands and squeezed as hard as he could, saying, 'he's a really big guy, you know, you should watch out . . .' without ever saying who 'he' was. But there were things which were even harder to take than all of that."

The cruelest tactics are often the more subtle, and the day that his torturer made him this strange offer is but one example: "I swear to God," he said, "that I will stop beating you if you hit yourself hard in the face."

"They do everything they can to make you feel that *you* are responsible for your own demise," Arya explains.

After yet another refusal, the interrogator begins to get annoyed. "It doesn't matter what you do, we'll beat you until you crack, one way or another. Why choose to suffer all of this for ten more days when you could be done with it now? Don't be such an idiot."

"Maybe he has a point," Arya begins to think to himself in a moment of weakness for which he can probably be forgiven, given the circumstances. It is not merely to avoid death that he hesitates. "Imagine not having anything to drink for days on end," he explains, "and then suddenly someone offers you a bottle of cold water. That's exactly how I felt at that moment. I was ready to accept ten hangings just to be allowed to sleep for half an hour."

The time soon comes for the final stage of his torturer's diabolical plan. He grabs Arya by the hair and pushes his head up against an adjacent door, through which he can hear another man in the middle of confessing that he had tried to overturn the regime. "But . . . that's Mohammad. Mohammad!" he screams inside his head as he recognizes the voice of one of his most loyal comrades. A tear escapes from behind his blindfold.

"So, Arya," the interrogator smiles. "I wasn't lying, was I? You're all alone now."

The man sits his victim down once more, still blindfolded, and hands him a pen. "There's a name here. I want you to write down everything you know about him and his activities."

Once again, Arya will think long and hard about this in his cell but will not give in, thanks to his last remaining lifeline: his religion. "God helps those who resist," the journalist states frankly. This may seem strange, coming from someone who claims over and over that religion is the bane of his country. Finally, though, Arya's tenacity pays off. While still in isolation, he is transferred to a larger room, directly connected to the bathroom. The young man cannot help being a little disappointed. "My daily excursion to the toilets had become an adventure to look forward to, and now it was taken from me, although I can't overstate how wonderful it is to be able to go whenever you feel the need."

This new cell was also the stage upon which one of the happiest memories of his detention would be enacted. "My finger was broken from before, and I hadn't had time to take care of it before they brought me here. Because of the pain, they said that they would treat it for me and I had to slip my finger out through the gap under the door so that the guard could apply the cream. One day he just got sick of it and passed me the entire container. You can't imagine how much pleasure I took in reading the long list of possible side effects, over and over again for days on end. It was the greatest gift he could have given me."

After forty-five days in his *enferadi* (isolation cell), Arya claims one more victory and is allowed to call his family. The briefest of telephone calls—not more than a minute—conducted with his blindfold on. He was forbidden to say "yes" or "no," or to give any details about his detention or the reason for his arrest. "Pretty much all I got to say to my family, was 'Hi, I'm fine, good-bye.' That's not much after over two months without news, but I knew that they were happy to hear I was alive."

After the telephone call, the journalist is given daily walks in the open air. Twice a day, twenty minutes at a time, in a small alley about "thirteen to sixteen feet" long, these excursions allow him to retrain his eyes little by little. "I developed a technique. By raising the blindfold up a little and squinting with my eyes, I could make out shapes forming around me. I cried with joy when I saw that I was no longer alone. I was in the land of the deaf, but I was no longer alone." A land of silence where no prisoner dared even whisper, knowing that two days of harsh interrogation would be the punishment.

Five times a day the radio was turned on for prayer and, of course, for the supreme leader's speeches. "You pray for them to leave it on, to give you something to tear you from your solitude. But the very second that the speech finishes, the guard flicks off the radio, leaving you simply dying to hear just one second of some other program, even a commercial."

For the first time, Arya hears another prisoner's voice. He hears the pained screams as this person is taken down the corridor, and he can tell that the man is afraid of death. He will later learn that the prisoner in question had been there even longer than himself and that he had thus far resisted as well. Faced day after day with his relentlessness, the torturer had told him that he would be executed, even going so far as to help him draw up a will. This was still not enough to make him give in.

The next thing to change for the prisoner is the quality of his meals. He looks at the gap under the door one day to see a succulent *ghormeh sabzi* waiting for him. "I was so happy. I spent hours looking at the first spoonful, savoring it before devouring the whole thing. When I finally put it in my mouth, however, the stew wasn't even cooked."

Little by little, even his interrogator's attitude begins to change. "What will you do if you are freed?" he asks.

"I don't really wish to answer that," Arya dares to reply, feeling the strength returning to his wings, which are preparing to spread again. The man smiles. Arya did not need to tell him anyway, for after sixty-two days of solitary confinement in Evin Prison's 2A wing, under the exclusive control of the Revolutionary Guard's intelligence services, Arya is now transferred to the public section of the prison. His blindfold is taken away for good. The light is blinding, but at least this time it is daylight. The cell is large and there are three other prisoners, a television set and—what luxury—a pile of reformist newspapers (well, the two that are still in circulation).

"I was free," he beams joyfully. The light in this cell is also left on throughout the night, but this time it is not to torture the cell's inhabitants but rather to film them. Each and every prisoner here is locked up for political reasons, and they have been brought in from various prisons around the capital.

"We felt as if we had each come from a different country. We laughed, we supported each other," Arya reminisces. It is common knowledge that at Evin, the prisoners are allowed to speak to one another and share stories. Among this group is Emad, a twenty-one-year-old Kurdish man, arrested for dealing speed. His product confiscated, he was sent to prison, not in Evin but in Kahrizak, the mere mention of which is enough to make many young Iranians shudder.

Although previously reserved for the lowest criminals from around the country, many protesters arrested from June 2009 onward were sent there by the police, often in complete anonymity. More focused on enjoying their loot, the three officers sped up Emad's admittance to the infamous prison by labeling him a protester, and the young man was made to pay dearly for this unfortunate error. There it is not blindfolds but rather a bag on the head, plastic disposable handcuffs, and three days in a container cell without food, water, or the opportunity to use a toilet.

"It's like being in the Middle Ages at Kahrizak," Arya explains. "Evin is a paradise in comparison. These guys were piled in, one on top of another, and given nothing but scraps to eat. Even animals would get more respect." Emad had an interrogator of his own, although his was far less subtle than Arya's.

"He wanted him to admit that he had set fire to a mosque," the journalist reveals. The Kurd was beaten, tortured, and sodomized multiple times with a billy club. "They even held his head underwater in a bowl that they then electrocuted." But Emad, like Arya, did not crack.

Until this point, Kahrizak's very existence had been kept a secret. "Dozens of murders have taken place there with complete impunity for the perpetrators. So many anonymous young men have disappeared in this way." Arya states.

The jailors even once attacked the son of an ultraconservative, and it was this tragic death which finally caused the Kahrizak scandal to erupt. Twenty-five years, old Mohsen Ruholamini was the son of Abdol-Hossein Ruholamini, close advisor to Mohsen Rezaï, former head of the Revolutionary Guard and conservative candidate at June's election. Despite his father's position, Mohsen himself took part in street demonstrations to reclaim his vote, convinced that the count had been rigged. On July 9, 2009, he was arrested not far from his home. The police contacted the family, telling them not to worry and reassuring them that his father's standing would ensure a quick release. Two weeks later, however, Mohsen's parents were summoned to collect their son's corpse, his body mutilated and jaw broken. Saeed

Mortazavi, the capital's prosecutor who boasts the nickname "the Torturer of Tehran," would later announce that the boy died of meningitis. Just one month later, a court police report made public by the governmental agency Mehr would confirm that the young Mohsen Ruholamini died for reasons of "physical stress, [caused by] detention conditions, [by] repeated hunger strikes," and by being "struck with a heavy object." The Iranian authorities, however, maintain that there has never been a death at Kahrizak.

Emad has spent time with several people who witnessed the murder. "Apparently," Arya relays, "after one particular incident, in which he had received particularly bad treatment from his jailors, Mohsen Ruholamini dared to shout out, 'You don't know who you're dealing with. I'm the son of Abdol-Hossein Ruholamini, and you're all finished.' In response, brigadier general Ahmad Radan, head of Tehran's police, threw a stone directly at the young man's head."

According to Mehr's information source, the victim was then transferred from Kahrizak to Evin due to his "unsatisfactory state of health," but was never admitted. He arrived at a hospital seventy minutes later and died there. Kahrizak's doctor, Dr. Ramin Pourandarjani, twenty-six years old, bore witness to these repeated episodes of torture and was ordered to provide an autopsy report to the effect that the prisoner died of meningitis. The doctor, however, took his own life on November 10, 2009, an announcement the authorities were quick to withdraw, stating instead that Ramin Pourandarjani suffered a heart attack upon waking one morning. The family was forbidden to carry out an inquest, and funeral services were carried out in the northwestern city of Tabriz, under heightened surveillance. On July 28, faced with a scandal of this scale, the supreme leader ordered that Kahrizak prison be closed.

Also in Arya's cell is a detainee who hails from a similarly heinous location, his devastated expression and frequent crying fits a testament to his experiences there. This man, one of the reformist camp's key players, is also a former resident of the 2A wing and was under the full responsibility of the Revolutionary Guard. It was he who Arya heard screaming from his cell. "He was terrified. Afraid of the death warrant he had just signed and afraid of the trial that would follow. As he refused to talk, the interrogator made good on his threats, savagely beating the man's son in front of him."

The final cellmate, a young nineteen-year-old, barely talks. His face is vacant, traumatized, and he looks close of death. As soon as Arya tries to find out where he was before, the boy begins to shake and works himself up almost to the point of nervous breakdown, which his new friends try to calm with their understanding embraces. The boy was not always this way and was once brave, courageous, with a thirst for life. Several weeks away from taking his place at a prestigious university, it was he who encouraged his friends to take to the streets the day after the election. He attended every demonstration but was finally captured on a cell phone video, filmed close up shouting antigovernment slogans. The video was played that same night on a well-known foreign television station and, after seeing the images blown up on the screen, the young man had no choice but to flee to the provinces. It was not long, however, before the Ettelaat caught up with him.

"As soon as they got hold of him," Arya recounts, "they beat him and pushed him into a hole that they had dug out with a shovel. The space was so small that he couldn't even lie down. The agents filled the hole in with earth, leaving him just the tiniest of openings to breathe through. The boy spent ten days there."

His torture finally over, he was taken to Tehran and thrown into an isolation cell in the wing of Evin prison under the control of the Iranian intelligence agency. "Because the Ettelaat are secret service employees, they act out of self-interest and ignore the teachings of their faith," Arya explains. The boy was locked up for an entire month before being sent to Evin, and he is now banned from studying for the rest of his life. "Most of all, he doesn't want to even hear mention of the protests."

Sandals are heard again during the night, waking Arya with a start. A guard knocks at the door and asks the journalist what size he wears. The following day, he returns with a light blue suit, and orders Arya to dress immediately.

"You're lucky, kiddo. You know how many people dream of being on television?"

Without any further explanation, he passes him his old friend, the black blindfold. Emad, the Kurd, hugs the cellmate who has quickly become his best friend, offering him strength, then watches as Arya leaves the cell and is led to a truck waiting outside. The journalist knows full well where he is being taken, but is unclear as to what may be waiting for him there.

"I had heard in the past of these trials. My comrades had explained to me that the accused read confessions aloud, confessions that were carefully dictated to them beforehand by their jailors. But I also knew that I hadn't received any prior coaching."

They remove his black blindfold. At this August 25 trial—the fourth in less than three weeks—dozens of accused, all dressed in the same "light blue pajamas," are offered up in front of the flashes and video cameras of the state journalists. Among them are some of the greatest reformist figures, rounded up the day after the elections. Saeed Hajjarian, former advisor to reformist President Khatami and one of the brains behind the movement; Mostafa Tajzadeh, Mohsen Aminzadeh and Mohsen Safaei-Farahani, former deputies; and Abdollah Ramezanzadeh, former spokesperson for the Khatami government. The prosecutor reads the charges, including, "acting against national security," "casting doubt on the election results," "being in contact with British secret services," "spreading antiregime sentiments and ideas," and "insulting the supreme leader."

"I carried out a false analysis of the election, and this was a huge mistake," Saeed Hajjarian, one of the Green Movement's key figures, paralyzed after a 2000 assassination attempt, tells the court. "I ask the Iranian nation for forgiveness in the light of the damaging actions which resulted from my false analyses."

Arya feels his blood begin to boil. "I just can't believe it," he moans to himself. "What can they possibly have done to him to make him deny his entire existence like that?"

Mir-Hossein Mousavi will later denounce these "show trials" and confessions "obtained under torture." Hajjarian declares his resignation from the reformist party Mosharekat and announces that he now "stands alongside the Constitution and the supreme leader." Once his confession is over, the judge rules that Hajjarian be given the maximum sentence. Given the accusations and the strength of these confessions, the accused runs the risk of being hanged.

Two hours later, Arya is taken back to his cell to the great delight of his comrades, who take him in their arms. After seventy-five days of detention in Evin, the young man will finally be freed, almost twenty pounds lighter than before. This did not come cheap. His family had no choice but to remortgage their home in order to raise the 200 million tomans ($200,000) required for his bail.

22

"FROM NOW ON, all protesters will be treated as Israeli spies." This was the announcement made yesterday by the Revolutionary Guard, a month after the Iranian people last took to the streets. In all likelihood, this quiet period can be explained by the revelations of torture cases and repeated prison rapes, as well as by the show trials in which numerous young protesters and key reformist figures have been seen on television making peculiar confessions. Today marks the occasion of Tehran's traditional Jerusalem Day. Each year, the regime brings together thousands of its supporters, bussed in with the promise of free fruit juice and vast television coverage, and shows the rest of the world, through its pro-Palestine—or more importantly anti-Israel—rallies that it has the support of its people. For several weeks, the opposition has been using the Internet to send out a call for its supporters to use this date as an opportunity to take to the street again. Could it be that the Green Movement has suddenly decided to swear allegiance to the regime?

"We have entered a new phase," Arya, who has gained back a few of those pounds he lost in jail, explains in an email. "And we're calling it the 'Great Hijack.' By infiltrating the official procession with our protest, we should be safe from any violent repercussions."

"Death to America," an aging man with a black beard shouts into a microphone.

"Death to Russia," the crowd responds in unison. Surprised and wondering whether he might have misheard, the man tries again.

"Death to Israel."

"Death to Russia," (the Islamic Republic's greatest ally) the crowd continues.

We are now on Karim Khan Avenue, where tens of thousands of Iranians have convened, forming the largest gathering since June. In the crowd is a newcomer, a young twenty-four-year-old, smiling from ear to ear and timidly joining in with a few of the slogans. It is Reza, and today he is on foot.

"*Mashallah*," the taxi driver beams. "This is my people. This atmosphere is just unbelievable." He is right; it feels like an eternity since June's bullets rained down on his fellow men and women.

Behind the official flags of the Islamic Republic, a few families continue to chant their timeless revolutionary slogans, which must take some courage, surrounded as they are by thousands of green protesters. Perhaps the two sides really can live together—happily even—coexisting without hostility. There is at least one man, though, who cannot take it anymore.

"*Baba Hadji* [a respectful term for a pilgrim who has recently returned from Mecca]," he shouts to the amusement of all, "can't you change the station?"

The huge crowd now reaches the Karim Khan Bridge, swallowing up cars and their ecstatic occupants. In one of these cars are Azadeh and her mother. "I love you all," the younger woman screams from her open window. All of a sudden, a biker stops his motorbike a few feet in front of them, steps down from his vehicle, and abandons it right there in the middle of the street. A chorus of car horns responds.

"*Baba*, are you nuts? Can't you see the line here?" one dumbfounded driver cries. "Come back and get your bike."

The biker turns round and shouts back, "*Dadash* [bro]. Park yours too and join the people."

"The people of this country are *jav guir* [lead by their emotions]," Arya smiles, "for better or for worse."

The police are also present at today's gathering, as are the Basijis, who are tearing round on their motorbikes, flexing their muscles in front of the crowd. Each time they come into view, they are met with boos from all around but, to everyone's surprise, no punishment is dealt out.

"Hoda, Hoda . . . get down here right now, and bring your friends," Azadeh cries into her cell phone to her best friend, unable to contain her excitement. "It's amazing, they're not attacking anybody, hurry up."

Text messages may still be blocked, but phone calls are getting through at least. A few minutes later, the young woman also decides to abandon her vehicle, fearful of missing even a minute of today's spectacle.

Just a few moments ago, the ultraconservative Ayatollah Ahmad Khatami made his announcement. "There are two main reasons for which we support Palestine and Jerusalem: first of all, because all Muslims are part of one unique nation and secondly, because we stand by all who are oppressed. The Zionists have tried to turn our Jerusalem Day into a failure, but they will not succeed." Here he speaks the truth, for today is anything but a failure.

"Not Gaza, not Lebanon, I'll sacrifice my life for Iran," the crowd screams from Karim Khan Avenue.

"Not Gaza, not Lebanon, I'll sacrifice my life for Iran," Reza repeats.

The people have spoken, referring here to the astronomical sums transferred by the Iranian regime to Palestinian Hamas, as well as to Lebanon-based Hezbollah.

"But no, hang on," Azadeh tries to interrupt. "In Iran as well as Gaza, put an end to all the murder." Her words are met with silence from her fellow protesters.

"Your slogan sucks, honey," her mother shouts, followed by laughter all around.

Worried that despite his microphone he is about to lose control of the situation, the elderly man from earlier moves on to a different chant.

"*Allahu Akbar.*"

"*Allahu Akbar,*" the crowd cries itself hoarse. The man can breathe again; he has regained the respect he was looking for. His tactics may have been a little sly, but he is certainly not the only one at today's event using his cunning to get attention.

Television stations are broadcasting live images of the huge gathering, filmed from helicopters overhead. "The Iranian people took to the streets today in the millions to show their solidarity with the Palestinian people who have been under Israeli occupation for over six decades," the commentator takes great pleasure in announcing. "They have also gathered in huge numbers in the cities of Bushehr, Rasht, Tabriz, Isfahan, Shiraz, Ahvaz, and Mashhad."

The Iranian people are not so easily duped. "We're used to being taken for fools," Azi explains.

Spotting the helicopter up above, the demonstrators wave their hands in greeting, brandishing their V for victory finger signs. Each person digs out some kind of sign—a banner, a ribbon, even their green nails—to show to which side they really belong. Some women are even spotted removing their green headscarves and waving them in the air.

"May dirt fall on my head to punish me for doubting my people and their solidarity," Azadeh sobs.[1]

"Tomorrow, I want everyone to get themselves down to the bazaar," shouts Mahnaz, a grandmother whose age nobody dares ask. "I don't want to see a single one of my children wearing anything other than green."

The people are not the only ones making themselves heard today. Their president—or rather the president put in place by the regime—has just made a thunderous announcement that only he can possibly explain, stating, once again, that the Holocaust is a "myth."

"The creation of this Zionist regime is based on false pretexts," he stated. "It is a lie based on a declaration that is both unproven and mythical." Opposite the University of Tehran, while the second-term president stands proudly for his interview with the state's second largest television station, he is suddenly interrupted by a series of cries behind.

"Ahmadi, Ahmadi! Resign, resign!"

This carnivalesque atmosphere should by no means allow people to forget the tragic destinies of Neda, Sohrab, Taraneh, and Mohsen, nor the hundreds, if not thousands, of protesters who are still locked up in the jails of the Islamic Republic. But they are far from being forgotten by their fellow countrymen, and their faces have been spotted multiple times throughout the crowds today, on giant portraits used by the demonstrators to mask their own identities.

"I swear to God that their deaths will not have been for nothing," Omid warns from Valiasr Square, before shouting toward a group of Robocops, "Confessions and torture won't affect us anymore," a cry quickly picked up by the rest of the crowd. It is hard to understand where this young man finds the courage to act in this way, but it must be noted that in this, he is not alone.

At the heart of the crowd, it is possible to spot no less than four of the opposition's main players, closely surrounded by their friendly bodyguards. The men in question are Mir-Hossein Mousavi, Mehdi Karoubi, former reformist President Mohammad Khatami, and also, to everyone's great surprise, the former moderate President Hashemi Rafsandjani, who has been lying low for the last two months. On top of this unexpected political support, the protesters are also backed by several key members of the clergy, notably Grand Ayatollahs Montazeri and Sanei.

"Montazeri, Sanei, here we have some real ayatollahs," the crowd chants from Valiasr Square.

The authorities need no more bait than that, and they descend into the crowd in reaction to this affront. In the middle of the group, former President Khatami is violently pulled to one side by Basiji officers on motorbikes. His clothes are torn and his turban rolls to the ground, but fortunately, the people are there to save him and they charge now at his attackers. Nonetheless, the reformist is forced to leave the march, and Mousavi and Karoubi—although not Rafsandjani—will suffer the same fate. The Islamic Republic's official press agency, IRNA, will later reveal that these figures were attacked by "angry mobs."

These "angry mobs" will not stop at the ayatollahs, and at certain spots throughout the capital this evening, pepper spray is used against the crowd. On Keshavarz Boulevard, Omid watches as dozens of protesters pull back and then begin to run toward him, causing him to fear the worst.

"*Khodaya*, I hope they haven't started killing again."

He need not worry this time though; it is "only" tear gas. As many women cover their faces with their headscarves, about a dozen protesters gather around one man in particular. Could it be that they have caught a Basiji? The man is puffing on a cigarette, deliberately blowing the smoke directly into the faces of the crowd.

"Come on, hurry up," a mother shouts to her son, for this is no Basiji but a protester, and a good one at that. What he is in fact doing is helping to relieve the unpleasant side effects caused by tear gas.

"May God protect you, it really works," the mother congratulates him, despite the fact that this action means—technically speaking—that she, her son, and the other protesters have now broken their Ramadan fasts.

Around fifty police officers are stationed in front of Maryam Park, directly in front of Reza. Nervous as he is, he stares them down in silence, the memories of the shock he received in June flooding back to him. The officers suddenly move forwards in a line, getting dangerously close to the young taxi driver, a scene which could easily be mistaken for a pre-soccer-match confrontation.

"We're all the same," a man with a white moustache shouts. "Police officers, support us. Support us." He repeats this phrase, which is quickly adopted by the crowd, including Reza.

The day will end as it began, in a cheerful atmosphere, with only a few arrests and a handful of injuries. As the sun sets over Valiasr Square, the slogan which is carried into the evening sky is, "Dictator, dictator. This is our last warning. Iran's green people are ready to explode."

"By replacing 'Ahmadi' with 'dictator,'" Arya explains, "Ahmadinejad is no longer the only target."

Climbing into bed that night, Azadeh is conflicted. "I'm so happy. We needed this day more than anything, but I'm also afraid. Afraid because we really let loose there for a while and afraid because the Islamic Republic let us do it. I'm afraid because past events have shown us that manipulation is their forte."

23

"LIFE IS GOOD, DADASH [brother], don't you think?" Javad asks after taking a big hit of his hookah pipe.

"Shut up, *baba*, are you crazy?" Reza shouts in response. "Someone might hear us."

It is ten o'clock in the evening and the two Basijis are in a shisha lounge in the capital's southern neighborhood of Shoush, making the most of a few days of calm to relax a little. On tonight's agenda is a ferocious *Medal of Honor* battle, the PlayStation 2 war game that Javad has just treated himself to. Tomorrow's plan is the local swimming pool.

"*Dadash*, what's wrong with you? Chill out. If anyone has a problem with it, I'll deal with him myself," Javad responds.

June, with its massive demonstrations during which the two friends were constantly on the move, seems a long time ago now.

"It was a first for us," Javad explains. "But I think we came out of it as stronger people. We managed to hold back the rebel forces and our country has been saved."

Saved? But what about the recent Jerusalem Day protest, where the Iranian people descended once more into the street, in huge numbers?

"You can't call that a protest," the militiaman laughs. "It was more like a carnival . . . couldn't even have hurt a fly. Anyway, we were ordered not to act and we let the 'sheep' get it out of their system."

A group of friends who have also gathered in the lounge now stare at the Basiji, who scowls back at them in turn, causing them to immediately lower their eyes.

"Thanks to our *Agha* ['sir,' often used to refer to the supreme leader], we found the faith and courage to deal with these infidels and to enforce the rules of Islam in our country. Our leader was right, Ahmadinejad was the best candidate, the one to ensure that the country be run according to the Prophet's true, pure Islam. We have accomplished something too huge to even measure."

What does Javad think about the murders of his peers, among whom the names Neda, Taraneh, and Sohrab figure so clearly? "I don't think anything about it at all," he replies, dryly. "This is no place for feelings. Let them in and it's all over. Anyway, they were the ones who were starting fires everywhere, we just had a mission to carry out and we did exactly what we had to do."

The level of indifference is astounding. Perhaps it is due to the fact that Javad did not actually live through the experience of killing somebody with his own hands.

"But of course I killed some of them," he proudly admits, "and more than one, I'll tell you." The neighbors look over once again. "You know, we were taught not to feel pity, and if we had have done, then we would never have succeeded."

How about the children and grandmothers in the crowd?

"Like I said: no pity whatsoever. Mousavi didn't have to work them all up like that. He's the one to blame, not me."

Sitting opposite his friend, Reza—the same young man who infiltrated the crowd to stab someone in the back—cannot stop looking around. He is obviously not quite as at ease as his older colleague; perhaps not at ease at all. "I can't sleep anymore," he confesses. "I'm haunted by so many images. I'm the laughingstock of my neighborhood. I don't know what else to do."

"Don't say that," Javad interjects. "You're a hero and that's what you should be telling yourself. You had crowds of people, a whole army against you, but you did it, Reza, it was an amazing feat."

"An amazing feat?" the young man thinks to himself, before saying aloud, "We had weapons, Javad, *weapons*. Against people who had nothing, who were completely empty-handed. We're nothing but cowards."

Javad downs his boiling tea in one gulp before striking out violently at a cushion, making the neighbors jump. "What are you thinking, brother? If our leader hadn't given us weapons, they'd have stamped on us like you would a cockroach. And on Islam too. Is that really what you want? Protecting our religion requires sacrifice."

Reza cocks his head; he has not yet touched his tea. "No, of course it's not what I want," he replies. "I don't want to see Islam lose any more than you do, but look around. The Basij corps was originally created by Imam Khomeini to defend the country and the people. Our fathers were young men like you and me, and they were up against an entire world that supported Iraq. They didn't hesitate to run across minefields just to get thirty feet closer to the front line, and they did it all for their faith, for the imam, and for their love of their country and their people. Can you really tell me that we're like that today?"

The young group nearby is obviously delighted with the debate which they are witnessing, and their enthusiasm draws more threatening glances from Javad. Embarrassed by such frank conversation, he replies, "Don't underestimate yourself, brother. Do you think that just anybody could do what you do to maintain the sacred order, alone in the middle of thousands of people? We were protected by our faith, by our love for Agha. The blood that runs in our veins is an offering to our leader."

"Alone?" his friend questions him. "We weren't alone, brother. We had the entire police force, the Revolutionary Guard, and the Ettelaat by our sides. We had motorbikes, knives, and guns. You want to talk about faith? I saw faith in the eyes of those people who continued to demonstrate peacefully in the face of our bullets. I heard it all night long coming from the rooftops of the city, and it haunts me in my bed at night."

"*Khafesho, Reza* [shut the hell up]!" the militiaman cries suddenly. "You don't know what you're saying. These assholes dare to turn religion around to get what they want; they don't believe in anything. Look at all of these unveiled whores, all of these Los Angeles *bacheh soosool* [rich kids]. Is that what you want for our country?"

"And what about the grandparents, their grandchildren, the amputee war veterans," the younger man picks up. "You don't think that they've sacrificed things for their country too?"

The exchange provokes a few sniggers from the group seated on the neighboring rug. Javad leaps up, knocking over the sugar bowl, and pulls a sharpened knife from his pocket.

"What's so funny? You got a problem with something? Because me, if I have a problem, I kill it." Deciding not to get into a debate, the friends apologize and slip away as fast as they can.

Reza tries to pick up where they left off. "Javad, I'm not the only one who feels tortured like this, and you know it. Since June I haven't been able to look at myself in the mirror. You know that a good number of those kids would like to step down, at least for a while."

"Well, let them try, they'll suffer the wrath of the leader and all those who represent him." The Basiji is stubborn. "Let them try and you'll see, they'll be dishonored forever and banished for life."

"I'm not so sure," the teenager continues. "I've already been banished for life by my people."

The fury suddenly subsides, leaving room for a more tender tone to creep into the conversation. "Listen, kid," Javad whispers, "you are nothing in the eyes of your 'people,' as you say. Whatever you do, don't trust them. If they ever take power, you'll be locked up in a dungeon someplace. They'll take everything you've got, you and your family. Do you really think that when I shoot I'm not thinking of them? That I don't think of my mother or my sisters? It's thanks to me that they have something to eat at night, and it's thanks to our leader that today I am somebody."

"Well, I don't want this money anymore" is Reza's retort. "It stinks of the blood of innocent people. The entire country treats us like mercenaries, and I can't stand it anymore. I can't stand the way people stare at me in the street, at the market, even at the grocery store. You say they'll stick me down there to be forgotten? Think back to that day when Morteza found himself face-to-face with the crowd. They could have lynched him if they'd wanted to, but they protected him."

Javad twitches nervously as the conversation turns more serious. "I feel sorry for you, Reza. I didn't know that you were so weak. You have fallen right into the trap they set for you. Mousavi is the mercenary.

You've been fooled by the West. You didn't listen to Hamid's advice and let your feelings carry you away."

The older of the two friends takes one last hit of the hookah pipe before standing to leave. On his way out, he taps his friend nervously on the shoulder. "I love you, Reza, you're like my brother. But I have no other choice but to tell Hamid about this, it's for the best."

"Come on, bro, not that," Reza pleads. "I'm begging you, not that."

Javad drives home to play PlayStation on his own. As for Reza, he must suffer alone as he walks home to the sound of jeers and taunts coming from passing vehicles.

24

O N OCTOBER 1, 2009, having officially recognized Mahmoud Ahmadinejad as the winner of the presidential election, the United States, the United Kingdom, France, Germany, Russia, and China hold a meeting with Iran in Geneva to negotiate a halt to its nuclear program. As outlined in the agreement, the Islamic Republic would be required to send the majority of its uranium stock to Russia and France so that they may treat and enrich it before shipping it back to Tehran to be used as fuel in its research reactors. This is a historic meeting, as it brings together two of the planet's most rival countries—the United States and the Islamic Republic of Iran—as they sit down to their most important meeting in thirty years. During the luncheon, American delegate William Burns and his Iranian counterpart Saeed Jalili hold a private discussion lasting for around forty minutes.

Alone in front of the television set of his temporary country residence, Arya is beside himself. "We've just been struck with the biggest blow in our history." The young journalist collapses onto the Persian rug he uses as a sofa bed and bursts into tears. "I just don't understand. All they had to do was to say one thing, one sentence and our efforts would not have been in vain," he hits himself on the head. "What else do they need to show them that Ahmadinejad is *not* our president? We took to the streets to show the entire world what was happening, we let them arrest us, kill us, rape us, judge us . . . do they need us to start killing ourselves before they'll understand?"

"Dirt on their heads," Mandana screams at the bugs which are currently preventing her from watching the Persian-language BBC news in her house in Tehran. Every evening at nine o'clock, she and her daughter attempt to watch the shows broadcast by the British station, although often to no avail. "There are so many waves flying around in some neighborhoods of Tehran that you could use them to cook a chicken in just a few minutes," she jokes.

Tonight, the two women have no choice but to channel-hop through the radio stations available. All of a sudden, although not without great effort, victory is theirs as they succeed in tuning into Radio Farda, the opposition radio station. This is how they hear the news.

"Fools, cowards," Mandana screams, throwing an eggplant at the radio.

"Calm down, Mom," Azadeh tries to reason with her.

"Get away from me," her mother snaps. "Are they really this sadistic? So many of our children have been killed for *this*? A historic meeting? May God take them all."

Omid, in front of his plasma screen, laughs at the news. "Hey, I didn't expect anything less from the West. Everyone's in it for themselves, that's how it has always been and how it will stay." Pleased with this statement, the student continues. "You'd have to be blind not to see that Ahmadinejad is not the people's choice. When he was sworn in last month, he was flown to parliament in a helicopter to avoid the huge crowds that were trying to block his way." Omid tries out a little play on words which he just came up with. "Listen, it's not just our prisoners who were 'taken in.' Today the entire Iranian population has been taken as well . . . for a bunch of fools."

Arya is not so amused and is still in a state of shock. "How can you trust people who, on the one side, say that they don't want nuclear weapons because they are anti-Islam, but then on the other side, claim that June's presidential election was carried out legally? The West will regret this, and soon."

The West: a name which presses a lot of emotional buttons in Iran, inspiring deep admiration alongside intense disdain and frustration, feelings which took root at the beginning of last century when oil was discovered in the country.

"I love Alain Delon as much as I love George Clooney," Mandana confesses happily. "But you've got to admit it, the 'blue eyes' [Iranian nickname for Westerners] have been betraying us for a long, long time. And it's all just to steal our oil."

After their publicity peak in June—before they were outdone by the death of Michael Jackson—the opposition protesters have now been swept aside again to make room for the thorny debate that is the Iranian nuclear program.

"If they really believe that they will reach some kind of agreement"— Omid laughs again—"then they're completely fooling themselves. For four years Iran has been messing with them, trying to buy time wherever they can. This could go on for a really long time."

As disappointment sets in, it is time for a breakdown of the situation, and according to Arya, it is fair to say that the West has just committed "its greatest error in thirty years."

"They may not give a damn about the Iranian people," he continues, "but they really missed an opportunity here. By refusing to recognize Ahmadinejad, they would have put enormous pressure on the Islamic Republic and finally force them to change their behavior, in particular regarding the things they do which endanger the rest of the world. The West would have been the winner on every level, as the Iranian regime would have found themselves in a position of having to offer all manner of things in order to guarantee their peaceful survival."

The journalist goes on to underline one essential point. "You simply cannot trust Ahmadinejad. His kind—the kind that believes the apocalypse will come before Mahdi appears on earth—is not the kind of people who take easily to the idea of negotiating."

Now that Ahmadinejad's reelection has been officially accepted around the world, there must be a limit to what the West can do next. One possibility, which is looking increasingly likely, is a new round of sanctions.

"Sanctions have one victim and one victim only," Arya explains, "and that is the Iranian people, not the regime. They can only be effective if they are more targeted, for example if they go after the many assets held overseas by the ayatollahs and the Revolutionary Guard." He does have one other suggestion. "Put pressure on the Iranian regime to change how they honor human rights in Iran at the same time as dealing with the nuclear issue, as the two often go hand in hand. If Tehran doesn't keep its end of the bargain, then the West should sanction the Islamic Republic by placing travel bans on its leaders, by issuing arrest warrants or by repatriating its ambassadors. But the question is, is it in the West's interest to take things to these extremes?"

How about sending UN peacekeepers to Iran? "*Ghalat kardan* [It's not in their interest]," Mandana moans. "This is a situation which should be sorted out between the people of Iran. We know all too well that if they help us, they'll be back for a piece of the pie as soon as the regime has been overturned."

This is where one of Iran's greatest problems lies today. "The Iranian people will be on their own until all of their resources have been depleted," Omid grumbles, a hint of spite in his voice. "As for human rights, they couldn't care less."

Arya takes things even further. "The West will never allow the Iranian people to obtain democracy. Don't you see? With all of the resources we have here, in this idyllic geopolitical location, we would want to dictate our own oil prices and would quickly become a major force in the region. That is surely not in their interest."

With a president surrounded by doubt but internationally recognized all the same, with a forgotten people, and a nuclear program at the top of the priority list, the future looks bleak for the people of Iran.

"Don't worry," Azadeh smiles. "We're sick of all this talk. Nobody wants to help us? So be it. We know what to do. See you at the next protest . . ."

25

*H*EADS ARE BEGINNING to roll in the Islamic Republic. Think back to those reformist figures arrested the day after the election then judged in August in a series of public show trials. Their ordeal is far from over and their sentences have just been delivered. Each is given a hefty prison term for "endangering national security." Ali Abtahi, reformist former vice president, Mohammad Atrianfar, prominent journalist and close colleague of former President Rafsandjani, Behzad Nabavi, former reformist deputy speaker of parliament, and former deputy Ali Tajernia each received six-year sentences. Ahmad Zeidabadi, another renowned reformist journalist, was given five. According to Iranian state television, no less than 140 demonstrators have been brought to justice since last June's riots, and of that number, five were accused of taking part in the movement and sentenced to death and eighty-one ended up with prison sentences of up to fifteen years in duration.

A month after being freed, our friend Arya has still not stepped foot back at home. "It's the last place I can be safe," he explains. This young man is stubborn and even seventy-five days of detention were not enough to convince him to stop his activities. "Come on . . . have the people given up?"

Surely, though, he must fear being sent back to see his interrogator. "Not at all," he smiles. "I mean I'm not looking to die, but this is the price you pay in the Islamic Republic when you get involved in politics."

Just one week ago Arya had a pretty big scare. "Over email, a few of my colleagues and I had arranged a meeting at a secret Tehran location. Everything was planned down to the tiniest detail to ensure that nothing went wrong, but at the arranged time, no one showed up. It turned out that everyone else had been arrested the previous day."

Why everyone except Arya? "Honestly, I just don't know," he sighs. "Unfortunately, our problem lies in the fact that it's not just the intelligence services, at our heels. That would be easy, but on top of the secret services we also have the police, the Basij, and the Revolutionary Guard, the same people who arrested me the first time around. The problem is that each body is acting independently without sharing information with the others."

In this way, it is not uncommon for somebody to be released from prison one day just to be arrested a few days later by agents from a different force. "Many of my friends have had this unfortunate experience," the young reformist reveals.

Of course he himself is still only out on bail as he awaits his trial, and this could very easily see him sent straight back to Evin Prison. The boy, therefore, has been traveling around the country with great caution, staying with friends of friends but never with family. He keeps a maximum sum of 500,000 tomans (just over $500) on his person, along with a laptop and a bundle of other items, his razor not among them. He is convinced that the authorities are looking to arrest him once more. Having exhibited such composure so far, Arya starts to show the strain he is under.

"They pushed their way into my parents' home yesterday and went through absolutely everything. Sons of bitches, they even took my little sister away with them and interrogated her for a whole day before releasing her again." Luckily they did not go so far as to make good on the interrogator's previous threats, at least not for the moment. "They warned her that if I didn't turn myself in, they would not be so kind the next time. They're worse than ever."

So why does the young man not give himself up? "I'd turn myself in a flash if I could. I'm only two months away from prison anyway."

But he has just been given two bits of bad news, one on top of the other. The first, from the lawyer representing him in his case, was that if he were to be arrested again, he would be sentenced to a nonnegotiable, set prison term of ten years. The second, handed down from a friend who holds a position with a certain degree of authority, is worse still: apparently, the death threats made by the interrogator during his detention were more than a mere interrogation tactic.

"The authorities were really planning to execute me," Arya reveals coldly. "I was their best choice for two reasons: I was not well known enough for my death to cause the regime any serious problems, but I had a sufficiently large role to play that I would serve as a good example. Fortunately for me, a misunderstanding led to them not carrying it out."

So it is fair to say that today, the young man knows what to expect if he gets arrested again. The chase cannot possibly go on forever; as in a game of cat and mouse, the mullahs always come out on top, as he knows all too well. But how can he be effective in his mission if he is far from his people: overseas, behind bars or—worse still—hanging from the gallows?

It is with a heavy heart that Arya decides that he must leave the country, illegally of course. The main problem with his plan is one which is not to be taken lightly. His father was forced to remortgage the house in order to pay the bail which ensured his release from prison, but if Arya leaves the country, the house will forever remain the property of the Islamic Republic.

"Leave and stop asking yourself this stupid question," his father ordered him at their last meeting. His father is a religious man, and the house represents his only riches in the world. Nonetheless, Arya does as he says and decides to leave.

"I'm not running away," he asserts. "Being forced to leave your country in order to escape death and prevent your family's torture, do you call that running away?"

A good point, Arya, please accept our apologies. The plan is in place; the journalist must go. Before saying good-bye, or rather "see you later," his father gives him a large hiking backpack and some pistachios. He cannot provide him with his passport as this was taken from their home by the authorities, but even if he could, the boy would have no use for it, at least not on Iranian soil. A legal border crossing would be the equivalent of a one-way ticket straight back to jail. Instead, Arya will pay a smuggler 150,000 tomans and spend eight long days walking in the mountains before he reaches the border.

"What a feeling," he exclaims. "Was it freedom I felt? No way . . . it was the worst feeling I have every experienced in my entire life. In one second I left behind my country, my friends, and my family."

As the crucial moment is upon him, he throws himself to the ground, grabs a handful of soil, and takes in one last mouthful of Iranian earth. "It will always be a part of me," he says.

For security reasons, Arya will not reveal the details of his epic journey or of his final destination. "You wouldn't want me to shut down this route once and for all. It's a route that many of my comrades are forced to take on a daily basis." The journalist is right. By the time he was released from prison, the largest Iranian reformist newspapers, including *Etemade Melli* and *Etemad*, had vanished. As a result, almost two thousand journalists lost their jobs in less than six months. On top of that, there are the Iranians employed by foreign newspapers who were all forced to leave the country. Reaching the border does not mean that their perilous mission is over. In fact it is far from finished, as the Islamic Republic's agents are able to cross borders with amazing ease.

Once outside of Iran, Arya is haunted by his thoughts. "I'm nothing but a coward. Am I a coward? I shouldn't ever have left my country . . . was there another way? At least I know that my family is safe, but what will happen to my friends? What can I do to help now? What will become of my people? Will I ever see them again? I will . . . I'll see them again very, very soon." The young man tries to convince himself. "The protests will continue, and Mousavi will be president."

He begins to sob. "Even with a different president, those at the top of the regime will be the same, and they want me dead." Arya has never been one to bury his head in the sand, and he knows all too well that he will not be seeing his people anytime soon. The only way would be if the Islamic Republic were to fall tomorrow.

Night falls over this new, foreign land, but the journalist still has many miles to cover. Tonight the young reformer, a man with two thousand contacts who was set to be one of the great leaders of tomorrow's Iran, is alone and completely lost.

26

*A*T THE YOUNG AGE OF TWENTY-THREE, Majid Tavakoli is a well-known face at Amir Kabir University, perhaps better known under its former name of Tehran Polytechnic. But it is not his results which have earned him the respect of the entire campus. Universities in Iran are thought of as places of freedom; there are very few of them, but it was on their campuses that the Islamic Revolution, which eventually overturned the Shah, had its roots in the seventies. It was also from their grounds that the regime's greatest crisis surged—the greatest crisis until the 2009 protests, that is. Since Mahmoud Ahmadinejad's election as president, Iran's universities have been severely affected, providing a visible symbol of the oppression rampant throughout the country. The most politicized students are "graded" according to a star system which has nothing to do with their academic, the sole purpose of which is to exclude them from the establishments at which they are enrolled. The most secular—and often most brilliant—professors have been forced into retirement. None of this was improved by the ultraconservative's reelection in June 2009, and in September, the governmental press agency IRNA announced that all university programs would be Islamized.

Still, there remains one student at Amir Kabir whose star collection just keeps getting bigger. His name, of course, is Majid Tavakoli, and the current ultraconservative president was to learn this at his great expense. One December day, while making one of his famous populist speeches, the ultraconservative was interrupted by a shower of shoes which were thrown in his direction, along with several rounds of "Death to the Dictator" (the slogan making an appearance even at this early stage). It does not take a genius to figure out the name of the one person in the room who was brazenly unmasked, and as a result of the president's fury, the young Majid was sent off for a fifteen-month stay at Evin.

The charms of the individual holding cells, however, were not enough to throw the student off course, and as soon as he was released, he continued to spread his harsh criticism of Ahmadinejad's government through student publications. Yet again there was a furious reaction, and yet again he was arrested, this time spending two weeks in isolation. The young Majid's timing is impeccable, and he was out and in attendance for Mahmoud Ahmadinejad's reelection, as well as for every protest that took place in its aftermath.

If there is one thing the student leader cannot wait for, it is the start of the fall semester on September 23. Now that crowd gatherings are forbidden, it is the country's universities' turn to take the relay for the opposition. As a result, hardly a day has gone by over the last two and a half months—despite dozens of arrests—on which some kind of protest has not broken out on campuses in Tehran or elsewhere. It is not surprising that these demonstrations are taking place at the most prestigious public—and more politicized—universities, but what is new is that students at private Islamic institutions are also taking part, despite being under the strict surveillance of the intelligence services.

Once again, Iranian students will lead the way by daring to attack certain symbols which have thus far been considered taboo areas. On December 7, during Student Day 2009, hundreds of students from Amir Kabir ridiculed the Basijis who were filming them from the rooftops, waving 2,000 tomans bills ($2) in their direction.

"Khamenei, murderer, your regime is coming to an end," the students at another school dared to chant for the first time. Tehran's Khajeh Nasir University also had a glorious first as students waved an Iranian flag devoid of its central emblem, the symbol for the Islamic nature of the Republic. Worse still, on an unidentified campus— luckily for them—a portrait of the supreme leader was graffitied and then set alight.

On the occasion of this emotion-filled day, one smartly dressed young student climbs up to a podium at the Amir Kabir University campus and gives a speech to a thousand students, right under the noses of the Basiji militiamen in attendance. It is Majid.

"My friends, today is 16 azar (December 7). It is our day, a day for students. Today is a historic day for the student fight against despotism, and today is the day on which our nation demands freedom and vows to fight tyranny. Today is the day on which you have stood up alongside those who will not put up with this tyranny, to make your cries against dictatorship heard by all. My friends, my voice is not loud enough for everyone to hear. If we could only get hold of the microphone, there are many who would like, in your name, to address our country's tyrants and oppressors and to speak clearly and freely, to tell them that we've had enough of their autocracy. My friends, we will speak about the details later, but there is one important thing. Our first obligation—in honor of the efforts of our people who have taken to the streets over the last six months in the face of oppression, torture, and rape—is to gather at the entrance of the university and, one more time, to show our unity, our comradery, and our solidarity."

Majid will be arrested at the end of this speech, but his classmates have heard his message and, a few minutes later, are in position behind the entrance gates, the only way onto the street. The authorities, who have them under strict surveillance, have already locked the gates, and the trapped students now try to break through the barricade.

"Don't be afraid, don't be afraid. We have each other," they shout in chorus.

In the street in front of them, a mirror image of the scene is taking place as protesters there attempt to pull down the gates in order to gain access to the campus. During this spectacle, the Basijis are careful to film as many faces as possible.

"Film this, asshole," one student yells to an officer, waving a V for victory finger sign in his direction.

The gates finally give way and there is much excitement all around. This is an important symbol: the street freeing the university (or perhaps the other way around, it is hard to tell). Student slogans fill the air, almost an exact reenactment of a scene played out thirty years ago, which ended with the fall of the Shah.

The following day, the government agency Fars News, closely associated with the Revolutionary Guard, will publish a photo of Majid Tavakoli dressed in a black chador. The press agency explains that the student activist hid inside women's clothes in order to escape the forces and flee the campus. The testimony of several students present at the scene, however, was that their leader was not wearing a chador at the time of his arrest. There is no doubt in the students' minds: The photo published by Fars was intended to humiliate Tavakoli and to discredit him. As proof, the governmental agency publishes another photograph alongside that of Tavakoli, this time a mug shot of Abolhassan Banisadr, the Islamic Republic's first president from 1980 to 1981, also sporting a chador. Banisadr was accused at the time of dressing as a woman in order to escape the country after his 1981 impeachment.

If there is anyone on whom the Iranian people have learnt they can rely over the last six months (apart from one another), it is their fellow countrymen overseas. A mere few hours after the photo was published, an overwhelming number of diaspora sweep through Twitter and Facebook to turn the joke around on the Iranian regime. With the help of some talented models, they offer up a collection of photos of Iranian men, dozens of them, all dressed in chadors or in black, flowery, or green headscarves, often accompanied by a V for victory. The outfits are donned by anonymous models, children, but also renowned professors, such as Hamid Dabashi at Columbia University or Ahmad Batebi, an exiled Iranian student in the United States, now a symbol of the 1999 student demonstrations. The site iranian.com, one of the most popular sites among the diaspora, launches its campaign, *Be a man*, calling for its readers to send in photos of themselves dressed in chadors and to upload them to their Facebook profiles.

These expatriate Iranians do not stop there. Spotting a perfect opportunity to warm the hearts of their fellow countrymen from afar, they decide, thanks to a little assistance from Photoshop, to deck out Supreme Leader Khamenei and even President Ahmadinejad himself in the famous chador. Majid Tavakoli's chador quickly became an Internet sensation, pushing the student leader—who asked for none of this—to iconic opposition status. Music videos featuring dozens of veiled men begin to surface. As a symbol of solidarity with the young Iranian, the majority of men photographed chose not to hide their faces, despite the risk that they would never again be able to set foot on their country's soil. Many people also point out that the campaign pays homage to the Iranian women who have found themselves, since the advent of the Islamic Republic, forced to wear the veil throughout their entire lives, and who have been "considerably degraded" by the whole affair.

Neda and Sohrab can rest in peace, for they now have a new ally at their side, an ally whose courage is never ending, and who has substantial backing from overseas. As a testimonial, the last message that Majid Tavakoli posted on his Facebook page, two days before his arrest, read as follows:

> Just two days left [before Student Day]. I have spent ten exhausting days traveling for over one hundred hours, and now I must head to Tehran. My mother's eyes are filled with tears, and I see the anxious expression on my father's face, but despite this, I know that the only thing which can drive me on and keep me safe is my vow for freedom. Once more I welcome and accept the dangers, standing alongside the friends with whom I am honored and proud to spend 16 azar (December 7); shoulder to shoulder, as we speak out against tyranny, and for freedom.

27

MULTIPLE FIRES BURN UNDER the Kalej Bridge in Tehran, darkening an already dull December sky. "Death to Khamenei. Death to Khamenei!" is the cry from hundreds of Iranians, marching forwards hand in hand.

Today commemorates Iran's annual Day of Ashura, the anniversary of the martyrdom three thousand years ago of Imam Hossein, an idolized figure who has become a symbol of antidespotism resistance. Each year, the Iranian people mark the occasion by taking to the streets to show their faith in Shiite Islam. Every mosque in the country organizes *tekieh*, processions at which men can be seen carrying out traditional self-flagellation rituals, while members of the younger generation hold "Hossein parties," making the most of one of the year's rare opportunities to enjoy themselves throughout the night. In today's crowd, however, there will not be many people carrying whips.

Six months after the widely-contested reelection of Mahmoud Ahmadinejad as the country's president, the Iranian opposition has decided, once again, to employ its hijack strategy and infiltrate an official commemoration in order to make its voice heard. This time, however, the reformist camp's leaders will not be present. Under the Kalej Bridge, Azadeh has kept her promise, as has Mandana, who is at her side again.

"This holiday is our only ally," she smiles emotionally. "Because Ashura is one of Shiite Islam's mourning symbols, anybody who spills blood on this day is considered *haram*."

Her mother is not the only older woman present today; in fact those that have dared to defy the government are greater than ever in number. Much like Mandana, many of them have made it a point of honor to bring their sons and daughters along with them, and the majority of these children are considerably younger than Azadeh.

"Death to Khamenei. Death to Khamenei," they chant.

It is hard to believe this incredible scene. Even just a few weeks ago, this expression was still a huge taboo, although many Iranians thought it loud and clear in private. To pronounce it in public like this could earn them life imprisonment at least, if not the death penalty.

"*Dameshoon garm*," Azadeh weeps. "For thirty years this has been bubbling away in the pits of our souls, but today it is going to explode . . . The Iranian people have done it. The wall of fear has come crumbling down."

"This is the month of blood, Seyed Ali will fall," the crowd now shouts.

"Moharram month is often called 'the month of blood,'" Azi explains. "As for Seyed Ali, I'm sure you know who they're referring to . . . [Khamenei]."

Once again, the protesters are not alone. Javad, with his motorbike, his red helmet, and his revolver, sits just a few streets away, waiting patiently. There has been no sign of Reza, but Javad has other things on his mind as he listens intently to the insults directed at his idol, thanks to whom he owes his current job security.

"They're showing their true colors now," he scoffs. "Just like I said, they're nothing but a bunch of low-life rioters." Engines in first gear, muscles flexed, and the line of twenty motorbikes sets off.

Gunshots are heard not far from the Kalej Bridge, followed by a long silence then screams from women around. A crowd gathers around a man laid out on the ground. He must be about sixty years old and a woman leans over him, trying to tend to his wound.

"*Ey khoda* [Oh my God]." She holds her head in her bloodstained hands. "They're killing the people. They're killing the people." The protester's body is held up in the air.

"I'll kill him, I'll kill him. I'll kill the man who killed my brother," the cry rises up from the street, followed by, "Khamenei. Murderer. Your time is coming to an end."

"What savages," Mandana cries. "Do they have no faith at all, no dignity? There is nothing Islamic about this regime. It's nothing but military tyranny." She grabs her child by the arm. "Come on, my girl, it's time to go, I don't want to lose you too."

Azadeh spins around. "No, Mom, it's my duty to stay. As for you though, I order you to leave. Go home, this is no place for you."

Mandana pulls her daughter to her. "I love you, *azizeh delam* [my heart's angel]."

"Khamenei, shame on you. Set your people free," Omid and Kian sing together from behind their protest masks in Valiasr Square. Thousands of people have besieged the area, pushing back the outnumbered Basijis and police forces.

"Long live Hossein. Mir-Hossein. Long live Hossein. Mir-Hossein," they now shout like a crowd of soccer fans. It would appear, on this day of mourning, that the imam is not today's center of attention after all.

"We are all Neda. We are all Sohrab. We speak in one united voice," Omid screams, repeating his slogan with *jav guiri* (excitement).

"It's incredible," Kian continues. "We are reliving history. Look around you, listen to these slogans. Despite all of the repression we have suffered, there are more people here than ever before. No one cares about Ahmadinejad today, it's the leader's head they're after."

"Rapist. Murderer. Death to this regime," he chants now, his words quickly adopted by the crowd.

Suddenly, shots ring out around the square, causing general panic and commotion. It sounded like they came from the roof of a neighboring building or perhaps from the police station a little farther down. Either way, two men are down. One of them, a teenager, lies in a pool of blood, a hole visible in his leather G-Star shirt; he was killed by a sniper bullet in the back. Not far from where his body lies, the other boy was luckier. He is writhing around on the ground but was only hit in the leg.

"Don't be scared, son," a stranger comforts him. "You'll live."

Noticing the cell phone which is filming him from above, the victim smiles and raises his hand weakly, forming a V for victory with his fingers.

"Oh, treacherous leader, may you be banished from this land. You have ruined our country's soil, you have killed our nation's young people. *Allahu Akbar*. You have wrapped thousands of bodies in your shrouds. *Allahu Akbar*. Death to you. Death to you. Death to you."

These are the words of the revolutionary song struck up in harmony by hundreds of Iranians in Baharestan Square, in the capital's south. Amidst the women dressed in chadors comes a strangely deep voice.

"*Mashallah* to my people," shouts Reza, visibly having the time of his life.

The crowd changes tunes. "Obama, Obama. *Ya ba ouna ya ba ma* [Obama, Obama. Make your mind up, it's either them or us]."

The taxi driver, overcome with emotion, picks it up happily. "*Eyval* [Bravo]. I guess my slogan was outdone . . . Long live Iran, long live the Persian people." Here too, the special police forces are quick to bare their teeth.

"*Yallah, yallah*," someone bellows from far away.

The crowd disperses, but one mother, caught in the trap, struggles to run and finds herself trapped in front of half a dozen officers. Showing no mercy, they charge toward her, managing to corner her in a narrow alleyway. Beaten first with sticks then with billy clubs, they cannot quiet her distress calls, to which her fellow protesters finally respond.

"Savages, leave her alone!" around fifty demonstrators, stones in hand, shout as they hurry toward the police officers.

"Wow, hooray . . . *Barikala* [Bravo]," a delighted young woman shouts in excitement at the assailants. "We've cornered them!" The Robocops have no choice but to release their prey and run for their lives.

Another fire has started in the Kalej neighborhood, and this time it is a 250cc motorbike which is burning, and which will soon extend its flames to a nearby building. The cries are deafening.

"Where does our oil money go? In the Basijis' pockets!" the crowd wails.

"Bullets, tanks, Basijis, they don't affect us one bit," Azadeh, her mother, and everyone around them jump for joy, pulling off their headscarves as they dance.

It is utter chaos; trash cans are overturned to form barricades here and there before being set alight, and the curb is being smashed up, its pieces used as projectiles. Suddenly, a crowd gathers to the left.

"Bully, traitor, mercenary," comes the cry from dozens of protesters. "You kill your own people, just like that?"

As you may have guessed, they are surrounding a Basiji officer, the owner of the burning motorbike, whose face is covered in blood.

"Here, take that. That's for Neda," a young man screams as he strikes him violently across the face.

"Murderer," an elderly man chimes in, hitting him in turn.

All of a sudden, a female protester clad in a green headscarf jumps between them.

"Don't hit him, I beg you," she cries. "Don't you see that this is exactly what they expect from us? This boy is our brother, leave him alone." The beating continues.

"Leave him alone, leave him alone, leave him alone," the crowd picks up the chant.

The woman's pleas are finally heard, and the militiaman—terrified at this point—is released. His savior, however, has not finished with him yet.

"Undress him," she orders.

With the help of her peers, the young woman begins to remove the soldier's clothing, one item at a time, until he finds himself in nothing but his underwear.

"Go girl, I love it," Azadeh applauds as she jumps up and down with glee. The female protester holds the red helmet up as if it were a trophy and is praised by the crowd.

A few minutes later, the mighty Javad emerges on his black motorbike, his gun at the ready. "The blood that runs in our veins is an offering to our leader," he shouts as he fires into the air. The crowd moves again but one demonstrator, slipping unnoticed through the people, manages to wedge a piece of wood into the wheel of the Basiji's bike. Javad flies through the air and hits the ground a few yards away, causing a wave of excitement.

"The blood that runs in our veins is an offering to our *people*," the crowd corrects his wording as they run toward him threateningly.

"How much did they pay you to attack us like this?"

Surrounded, the militiaman closes his eyes as he is attacked from all sides. His face and back already injured from the fall, Javad stays quiet. For the first time, he is afraid. Suddenly, though, he is picked up by three young men and carried by his feet and hands to the sidewalk a few feet away.

"Water, quickly, someone fetch some water," they cry. "Our brother is bleeding."

In Valiasr Square, the scene is beginning to look like the third intifada. Confronted with showers of stones thrown from the protesters, the security forces have been forced to abandon the entire intersection, and the police station—from where the shots were fired earlier—is now besieged by demonstrators. One young man climbs onto the roof before waving a black Moharram flag, on which is written *Long live Hossein*. The crowd claps and cheers in excitement.

"This is Hossein's army, Mir-Hossein's supporters," they cheer.

Lost in a cloud of smoke and tear gas, the demonstrators do everything they can to make themselves heard. Kian plays a *daf* (Persian tambourine) rhythm by drumming on the wall with his bare hands. A few minutes later, the police station is set alight to another round of deafening cheers. V for victory finger signs dominate the air above the crowd as two protesters use the fire to set light to a picture of Supreme Leader Ayatollah Khamenei.

"Death to the dictator," they shout, to the excitement of all around.

"Watch out," comes the sudden cry from Omid. A police vehicle, unnoticed until now, is accelerating and charging in the direction of the crowd.

"He must be crazy," Omid smiles. "Either that or he had too much to drink last night."

Close up, the vehicle looks a little strange. On both the front and back there are protective grates which act as shields. When no one suspects it, the pickup flips into reverse and charges backward, mercilessly running over several protesters. Agonizing screams rebound around the square.

"Assholes!!" Omid screams. "They crushed them!"

The protesters try to chase down the driver, who has already made a run for it; he will not be the only one to escape today. One of his victims, a young man covered in blood, is carried to a car by one of his fellow protesters. On the front seat is a woman holding a baby.

"Hurry, they're coming," one of the demonstrators warns.

"This is the month of blood, Yazid will fall," the crowd roars.

"This is surreal." Kian is in shock. "They're comparing Khamenei to Yazid, Imam Hossein's murderer and arch enemy of Shiite Islam."

The crowd has now come across an overturned police bus under the Kalej Bridge.

"Burn it!" they scream as Reza arrives on the scene to lend a hand to his peers. The police and other special security forces also have backup arriving at the scene, which could make for be a bloody confrontation.

"Fire," one officer commands.

Completely at their mercy, the crowd replies. "Oh, brothers, dear army brothers. Why are you killing your own men?"

"Fire, I said," the police officer repeats, losing his patience. Still no response.

"I would die for you, my brothers," Reza cries as the crowd rejoices. "Brave people of Iran, support us . . ."

Some distance away, Azadeh and Mandana, who have remained faithful to their post, are witnessing a unique occurrence. Dozens of special police officers, the infamous Robocops, have been driven back against a large grille by around twenty protesters. Huddled against each other, the soldiers attempt to hide under their helmets. A demonstrator points to one of them.

"Why do you do this?" he asks.

"I'm sorry," the officer replies, blood covering his face.

This time a woman jumps in, shouting, "You're just like Yazid. You *are* Yazid."

Completely bewildered, he mutters again, "I'm sorry."

The police are pushed farther and farther against the grille as one demonstrator pushes his way in front of the crowd to protect them.

"I'm not going to hit you," the first man reassures them, all the while capturing their faces on his cell phone.

"You and motorbikes," the woman starts up again, "you're "you're just cruel, nothing but a group of bastards." Tensions are running high, and the scene quickly turns to general pushing and shoving.

Under the Kalej Bridge, the crowd is still savoring its latest victory. "Down with the principle of velayat-e faqih [religious supremacy over politics, a founding principle of the Islamic Republic]." They are overjoyed. The demonstrators, by using this sentence, have found the courage to call for the separation of religion and politics in Iran, an idea which is being taken one step further a few hundred yards down, in Valiasr Square.

"Independence, freedom, an Iranian republic!" they shout, just one word away from the 1979 revolutionary slogan, "Independence, freedom, an Islamic Republic!"

Today has seen the people of Iran succeed in making themselves heard as much in the capital as around the country as a whole. Shiraz, Isfahan, Arak, Rasht, Mashad, Ardebil, Najafabad, and Tabriz also played host to large demonstrations.

But while the day may have ended on a positive note, with several victories under the protesters' belts, it is important to remember the sad reality: Thirty-seven people lost their lives, and almost one thousand five hundred were arrested. As usual, the Iranian authorities will shift the blame onto the good old "enemies" of the Islamic Republic; in other words the West and the People's Mujahedin of Iran, an exiled opposition organization.

While he may not have been in the streets himself today, Mir-Hossein Mousavi now joins the victim camp as his nephew Seyed Ali Mousavi is killed during one of today's protests. That very evening,

Mehdi Karoubi, the other opposition leader, will address the country's leaders through a condolence speech offered to the families of those who have disappeared.

"Even the Shah's regime respected Ashura Day . . . If you don't have religion, at least have some respect for freedom."

28

*S*HEYTOON (RASCAL) IS PROBABLY the adjective that would best describe Amir Arshad Tajmir. Like any self-respecting *pessar irani* (Iranian boy), Amir takes life by the horns. At twenty-four years old, the young man simply adores traveling through the magnificent countryside of his homeland, and upon returning to Tehran, he spends his evenings at the city's wildest private parties. Like Omid, he does not hail from a particularly privileged neighborhood. It is his handsome allure, along with his golden skin, long brown hair, athletic body, and wardrobe at the cutting edge of fashion, that earn the boy VIP invitations all over town. Many young Iranian men like to think of themselves as reincarnations of Paolo Maldini[1] and, at the moment, this particular one has the attention of four young women, each of whom see in him the man of their dreams. Not only is he the cutest guy around, he is also an extremely funny one, and like many of his peers, he uses his jokes to hide his daily frustrations. After a childhood haunted by bombs from the Iraq war, followed by an adolescence stolen by the mullahs and Basijis, the young man aspires to be free if nothing else. Last May, he happily allowed himself to be carried along by the gigantic green wave which swept the country.

"He doesn't care about Mousavi, Karoubi, or any of the others," explains Helya, a close relative. "All he wants is a better life, no matter which regime is in place." His family is not particularly politicized either. "We make the best out of what we're given," Helya admits.

His mother Shahin, however, is one of the star anchors on the government radio station Payam, which has been a source of conflict between her and her son in the past. "I don't want your money," he shouted at her one day. "It's *haram*, it's the Islamic Republic's money."

Several months later, however, once he had finished with his studies, his mother found him a job at her progovernment station. "He had to earn a living somehow," Helya justifies the decision.

Following the example of many of his friends, and led as always by his devastating sense of humor, Amir is quick to get excited about the presidential campaign. He cast his vote—there is probably no point in spelling out for whom—and as soon as the results were released, he did not hesitate for a second before encouraging his friends to join him in the street to ask, "Where is my vote?" Six months later, despite the murders and arrests, Amir has not missed a single demonstration, including the Ashura Day rally.

On Sunday night, Shahin receives a phone call. "Good evening, ma'am. I have the unfortunate job of informing you that your son, Amir Arshad, died today. He was run over by a bulldozer in the middle of a protest. Please accept our condolences."

His mother is dumbfounded. Her son was run over in the crowd? By a bulldozer? She wonders if she is having a nightmare.

"Please don't worry, ma'am," the male voice continues. "We have an ID on the vehicle. It was a black Nissan Patrol. We are currently looking for it and won't give up until we find it."

Still in a state of shock, Amir's mother calls the friends with whom he went to today's demonstration. She learns that despite going together, only one of them was by Amir Arshad's side during the event, and he does not seem very willing to cooperate.

"I'm not sure what happened anymore," he says. "I didn't get a good look . . . It was an unfamiliar car."

Shahin breaks down, and the boy finally tells her that Amir did not in fact die on the spot but on his way to the hospital. Even before they managed to get him inside the building, however, the police took his body, confiscating his cell phone before taking off.

What happened next? Phone calls; dozens of phone calls made to every one of the contacts in Amir's address book. Helya is among them.

"Good evening. Do you know someone by the name of Amir Arshad?" a husky voice asks. "All I want is to find out where he lives."

"I'm sorry, I have no idea," Helya replies, skeptical as to the caller's identity. "We're not very close."

The police then contact Ali, Amir's brother. After initially refusing to identify himself, the man on the other end of the line stops beating around the bush. "Come and identify your brother's body. It is in the morgue at Kahrizak Prison."

The young man begins to shake. The sinister prison may have been closed for the last five months, but the same is not true for its morgue, which still holds many a dark secret. Ali decides to get down there immediately.

"There was nothing left of his face," he recounts. "The car ran right over him."

It is the ring and the clothes worn by the boy that allow Ali to identify his brother. Beside himself with grief, he turns his attention immediately to the burial, which he will have to organize for Amir, a ritual which must take place before any commemoration service can be held.

Their timing as impeccable as ever, the police step in with one final blow. "That's okay, you can go home now, we will be in touch when it's time to collect the body."

The following morning, the entire Tajmir family gathers to comfort his parents, who are in a state of utter devastation, not helped by the lack of credible information made available to them by the authorities. Suddenly, on the television screen—which as always is plugged into the satellite—Voice of America begins to show the faces of yesterday's victims, among whom Mousavi's nephew. The next young man, his face covered in blood, is almost unrecognizable, but his long brown hair gives him away.

"It's Amir," Helya gasps.

Unbearable shrieking echoes through the house, but the worst is yet to come. A few minutes later, the station shows a video exclusive: a scene of many demonstrators fleeing Valiasr Square in an atmosphere of complete chaos. They are chased down by two police trucks, both armed with protective (or were they attack?) grilles. One of them suddenly flips into reverse, and women can be heard screaming as one man is pushed to the ground. The second truck speeds up, crushing the protester. The screams get louder and louder, and the vehicles vanish. The man is not moving; his face is covered in blood.

"They ran over him three times, the cars ran over him three times!" the amateur filmmaker shouts at the top of his lungs. "With police vehicles . . . police vehicles! *Ey Khoda, ey Khoda* . . ." The voice goes on and on.

At the Tajmir household, the wailing is even worse. "Our poor little Amir Arshad, our son . . ." they cry, not realizing that this is just the start of their ordeal.

For five days, the family will pay multiple fruitless visits to Kahrizak and make repeated phone calls in an attempt collect their son's body for burial. The video images, in particular the flashing police lights of the vehicles in question, speak for themselves: the authorities simply cannot deny it. But, of course, anyone who believes that has grossly misjudged the Islamic Republic.

"But no, ma'am, please calm down. This had nothing to do with us. That vehicle was stolen from us just the day before. Whoever did this decided to take it down to the demonstration, and we're sorry, but we just haven't been able to trace him yet."

"It was such a load of bull," Helya scoffs now. "But in the Islamic Republic, you have no chance but to suck it up."

Back in the prison reception area, one of the women loses her temper. "Look what they did to the young boy . . . all of that because he wanted an ounce of freedom? An innocent boy has left this world." The poor soul could just as well be speaking to a brick wall.

"We will be in touch" is their only reply.

Worse still, the day after her son's death, Shahin is suspended from her job at the radio station. After all, the show which she presents is a live broadcast, played around the entire country.

Finally, after six days, the telephone rings. It is the police, informing Shahin that she may come and collect her son's body the following day. Finally she will have some relief. Just two hours later, however, it rings once again.

"You must come and collect the body immediately. It is to be buried at five o'clock this evening, sharp." The authorities prefer to wait until the cemetery is closed before such ceremonies can take place.

"They're afraid of us," Helya snickers.

Two other protesters killed during the Ashura Day demonstrations—a young twenty-nine-year-old woman and a thirty-one-year-old man—will also be buried this Saturday, each in a different spot of the same Behesht Zahra cemetery. Unlike Amir Arshad, they at least were killed by bullets. As for Mir-Hossein Mousavi's nephew, he was very favorably treated in comparison, and his family was allowed to collect his body just two days after his death.

Amir's burial takes place at the far end of the cemetery, in a virgin lot void of other graves and forgotten by all. Only thirty members of his family and friends are authorized to attend the ceremony, including Helya.

"We were ordered to come in small numbers," she remembers.

Not that the Tajmirs are alone on this painful day. Over sixty members of the security forces, police officers, and plainclothes Basijis are also on the guest list, confiscating cameras at the entrance. A few yards away, at another virgin plot, a young woman sobs as she buries her husband, who also died on Ashura Day. Women in black chadors, presumably regime agents themselves, surround her and jeer, "Whore, this was all your fault. Cover your hair immediately."

"I was so angry." Helya feels her temper rising just thinking about it. "I wanted to tell them exactly what I was thinking. The worst part of it was that the woman was dressed perfectly correctly. My family begged me to keep quiet in case I gave the authorities an excuse to keep Amir's body from us." The family wins; Helya keeps quiet, and the body finally arrives. "He had already been washed," she explains, "as dictated by Islamic rules."

Shahin has stopped crying; she feels as if she is about to die. All of a sudden, the journalist throws herself onto her son's corpse and pulls at the shroud to get one final look at his face. She was not expecting the horrific sight with which she is met: Amir Arshad's head had been completely rebuilt, perhaps to hide the awful truth. Whatever the reason, the scene is terrible.

"Her cries were more like torture screams than tears," Helya remembers.

As the body is laid out amidst the crying and wailing, a woman in tears approaches one of the agents, a man of around fifty years of age. "Don't you have a wife? You can't have any children either if you are capable of doing this to our son."

Visibly embarrassed, the man whispers, "I swear to God, they make us do these things, of course we don't agree with them. They force us, ma'am."

Just one hour later, the family is asked to vacate the area. Even with Amir Arshad dead and buried, the authorities are not yet done with their harassment of the Tajmir family. Two days later, they are banned from holding a ceremony on the eve of the third day of his burial at the local mosque, an important tradition in Shiite Islam. The Tajmirs, however, have their means and the following day, after an intense round of the Persian equivalent of the game "telephone" (of which the people of Iran are masters), almost four hundred people will gather outside the home of the boy's aunt in order to pay homage to Amir Arshad. The aunt's address was posted on Twitter and among those gathered were many anonymous faces.

"What a beautiful sight it was," Helya recounts. "Shahin had dec-orated the room with flowers and placed photos of Amir Arshad all around. She was still in shock, but her pride came through."

"His name is etched in history," she must have said to comfort herself. "He died for freedom. He died a hero."

It could be seen as a victory for the family that on this Tuesday, not one single agent even showed his face (at least not in an official capacity). Of course, you can never be entirely rid of the police, and three days later, on the seventh day after Amir's burial, around thirty officers were stationed at Behesht Zahra. Same again on the eve of the fortieth day, a day on which Shahin's screams were louder than ever as she knelt on the Persian rug which covered her young son's grave. Next year, the anniversary of Amir Arshad's death will fall on the same day as the commemoration of the death of Imam Hossein, the symbol of Shiite martyrdom in Iran.

"The family doesn't care about that," Helya reveals. "Shahin is only now coming to terms with the fact that Amir Arshad has gone. She doesn't do anything anymore."

Whereas Sohrab's mother turned her son's death into a symbol of repression and a weapon in the fight against the government, Shahin does nothing but cry over her child. "Whether there's a regime change or not, nothing will bring back her son," Helya says.

These days, the radio anchor does not leave her home, although thanks to Payam's decision to rerun a series of older shows, her voice can still be heard around the country.

Amir Arshad, at least in the world of Facebook, is still alive. His profile, active and smiley as ever, introduces a handsome young man with romantic airs and cheerful words. Flicking through his photos, we see him having his hair braided by a beautiful young woman, practicing his breakdancing moves, posing next to a marijuana plant or bottle of Bacardi, or enjoying the beauty of a sand dune. In other words, your average guy. The most touching comments, however, are the remembrances from his friends, posted on his Facebook page the day after his death (December 27, 2009) and which seem, in some ways, to breathe life back into his lungs. They speak for themselves.

December 28, 2009, at10:10 a.m.
Sam Az: Amir, where are you?

December 28, 2009, at 12:24 p.m.
Sam Az: Shit, man! I can't believe it. May God keep you safe, Amir. I can't believe that you have left us, dear brother. But congratulations, you're a martyr :-(((((((((((((

December 30, 2009 at 10:16 a.m.
Iman Fz : The wind blows, inside tombs the wind blows, freedom will soon be here; and we will come out from the shadows.

December 31, 2009 at 4:57 p.m.
Shima Abdolahi: Amir Arshad? You've gone and left us, you jerk. You always asked me to keep in touch, not to leave without letting you know... Now you've gone off without doing the same! No, it's not true: You have given us a sign, a sign to the whole world. I can't believe it. Everyone was talking about you at school today - you're such a martyr that the entire university is talking about you! I'll miss you, a lot.

December 31, 2009, at 5:10 p.m.
Elena Eli: My beautiful friend, you have gone. You have slipped into a deep sleep. You have left this cruel world. I can't and won't believe it.

December 31, 2009, at 6:13 p.m.
Sam Az: My friend, it's been days since you became a martyr but I still can't believe that you've left us. I can't believe that my dear Amir, always happy and smiling, has left me alone so suddenly.

January 1, 2010, at 2:30 p.m.
Shima Abdolahi: Amir Arshad :- (If only your jokes were still here. :-(Get up!

January 14, 2010, at 1:31 p.m.
Parnaam Safavi: I miss you so much. Every time I asked you to put our photos up on Facebook you told me that soon I would get sick of you and only then you would post them. And now here I am today, commenting on your photo. I'm dying without you Amir, solitude kills me without you here, and I know my words won't change a thing. My darling Amir, I miss you.

January 18, 2010, at 10:51 p.m.
Sanaz Rashidfarokhi: May God help you :-(I made you a *shole zard* and I'm praying for you.

January 25, 2010, at 7:52 p.m.
Shima Abdolahi: I cried all night, when I awoke I realized I had been dreaming. What if it had been true? What if you had still been here? Will I only see you in my dreams now?

March 23, 2010, at 6:34 p.m.
Parnaam Safavi: My love, I went to your grave today and laughed so hard. You're not here but you still make me laugh, your photo was covered with tons of red lipstick marks . . . but now you're not here to make me jealous anymore . . . Crazy guy. My heart shrivels without you :-((I miss you so much!

29

*A*FTER ARRESTING DEMONSTRATORS EN MASSE, turning the streets red with the blood of its young people, and extracting confessions in Stalinesque trials, the Islamic Republic is ready to implement the next stage of its plan. This morning's news announces that two "demonstrators," thirty-seven-year-old Mohammad Reza Ali Zamani, and nineteen-year-old Arash Rahmanipour, have been executed by hanging.

"The men were members of the monarchist group Tondar [Kingdom Assembly of Iran], and admitted buying explosives and plotting to assassinate leaders," Reza Jafari Dolatabadi, Tehran's prosecutor, said in a statement.

These two "demonstrators" confessed on August 8 of last year during one of the aforementioned show trials, alongside French student Clotilde Reiss. They were sentenced to death in October as *mohareb*, or "enemies of God." Mohammad Reza Ali Zamani pleaded guilty but his lawyer argued for clemency, insisting that his client could not possibly be considered as *mohareb* because he was unarmed at the time of his arrest.

While the semiofficial press agency ISNA suggested that the executions were linked to the part the accused played in the prodemocracy riots, English-speaking Iranian state television station Press TV refutes these claims. They state instead that Zamani and Rahmanipour were executed following their involvement in an attack which took place in Shiraz in April 2008, killing thirteen people and injuring a further two hundred. Last year, this same station broadcast a video of the two men in which they admit having met with American and Israeli agents before carrying out the attack. Press TV is not the only source to contest the government's explanation.

Me Nasrin Sotoudeh, lawyer to the young Arash Rahmanipour, revealed that her client was arrested at his home in April 2009, two months before the presidential election, and that he was "forced to confess after receiving threats against his family." In an October interview with the news site Rooz Online, the lawyer explained that her client had "nothing to do either with the election itself or with post-election activities." Further, Me Sotoudeh stated in an interview with Voice of America that her client was still a minor when the alleged crime took place, and that he had been put under "incredible pressure" over the last ten months.

Even more concerning is the fact that, while Islamic law states that no verdict be carried out until it has been publically released, the lawyer reveals that neither she nor her client's family knew that he was be executed until after the fact.

"Just two days earlier," she recounts, "Arash had contacted his family and cannot have had any idea at that point about the verdict." She adds, "Arash's sister, who was pregnant, was arrested at the same time as her brother, and her two-month prison ordeal caused her to miscarry her child.

"The medical file as it stands," the lawyer continues, "was enough to throw out my client's case. There was obviously some kind of political motivation, which was allowed to influence the judicial process." She has not finished yet with her list of complaints about the trial.

"Contrary to the law . . . I was prevented from attending each and every one of the hearings and could not defend my client. In one such instance I insisted so forcefully that I was threatened with arrest myself. They took away my right to practice, and I was put under review. During this same particular hearing, Arash's father was also threatened with arrest. If Arash really was guilty of such a serious crime, would they need to put this much pressure on him?"

"The day of the hearing," Davoud Rahmanipour, Arash's father, told Al Jazeera in an interview, "I was informed that I could not attend and was handcuffed and arrested. The officers told me that if I wanted to be released, I should encourage my son to confess, that if he did so, they would make sure that his sentence was reduced."

Davoud Rahmanipour describes his son as an intelligent and optimistic young man with a deep love for his country. He refuses to accept any condolences, listening only to congratulations, given that his son is now ranked among the martyrs who died in the name of Iranian democracy.

Speaking from Tehran, one Iranian human rights activist stated that the accusations surrounding the young men's cases were "grotesque," especially given that "no monarchist organization has ever been registered under the name Tondar."

The lawyer's ordeal is far from over. The government spokesperson who announced the execution of the two men also revealed that a further nine "rioters" had been sentenced to death and were awaiting an appeals court ruling. Among them were two of her other clients, Ayoub Porkar and Reza Khademi, also accused of being *mohareb*.

"I fear that if they are subject to similar treatment, behind closed doors," she explains, "then their verdicts will be quickly decided, and that we will only learn of their execution after the fact." Tehran's prosecutor confirms that five of those sentenced were arrested on Ashura Day.

As the appeals court verdict is read out, it is announced that one of the accused, twenty-seven-year-old Mohammad Amin Valian, will be executed. This student activist is a member of Damghan University's Islamic society, a group which campaigned for Mir-Hossein Mousavi. The reason that this situation is so shocking can only be understood when looked at in relation to his crime: The young man was arrested after he was photographed throwing a stone on Ashura Day, December 27, 2009. According to conservative Grand Ayatollah Makarem Shirazi, anyone "desecrating" this holy day should be treated as a *mohareb*. The website nedayeh-azadi.org explains that the court in which Mohammad Amin Valian was judged referenced the grand ayatollah's speech during sentencing. Abdolfattah Soltani, however, a human rights lawyer in Tehran, declared that in accordance with Sharia law, the requirement for being categorized as *moharebeh* is absolute certainty that the person in question took part in armed activity, which is certainly not the case here.

Mohammad Amin Valian's case is unique in the sense that this is the first time that an execution has been directly linked to the protests, the first time that the Iranian regime has not fabricated links to "hypocritical" or "terrorist" organizations whose aim they consider to be the overthrow of the Iranian regime (royalist groups, for example, or those linked to the People's Mujahedin). The charges of which the young man stands accused include, "acting against national security," "campaigning against the Islamic system," and "insulting eminent figures of the Islamic Republic." According to nedayeh-azadi.org, Valian repeated during his trial that the three stones which he had thrown had in fact not injured anybody, although he did also admit to shouting "Death to the dictator" during a demonstration. Once his trial was over, he was taken immediately to an individual holding cell in the Revolutionary Guard's detention center (well-known by Arya, of course), where he still resides. Mohammad comes from a religious and revolutionary family and until now had never stepped foot outside the confines of Islamic law.

A heavy cloud has been hovering over the country since Ashura Day, and it is not only the demonstrators who have become targets of the Islamic Republic.

Reformists, journalists, students, feminists, religious figures, activists, poets, politicians, writers, professors, philosophers, translators, Bahais (a minority religion), bloggers, photographers, attorneys, architects, directors, lawyers, environmentalists, union members, ethnic minorities, musicians, as well as the wives, sons, and mothers of the above; all in all, no less than 223 Iranians (this list was compiled by Iran's international human rights campaign and is far from being an exhaustive document) have suffered at the hands of the regime.

The Islamic Republic has also sentenced certain defendants to heavy prison terms. The brave Majid Tavakoli has just been sent down for eight years for "insulting the president," "insulting the supreme leader," "participating in an illegal gathering," and "spreading propaganda against the system."

Reformists Mohsen Mirdamadi, Mostafa Tajzadeh, and Davood Soleimani were each sentenced to six years, the same outcome as that of Omid Motazeri, a twenty-three-year-old poet and journalist whose father was executed in 1988 and whose mother was arrested on the evening of Ashura Day. Hengameh Shahidi, journalist and member of the *One Million Signatures* campaign, was also given six years after she was found guilty of "antiregime actions, mutiny, gathering illegally, being a member of an organization which acts against national security interests, and insulting the president." Even worse, Nasrin Sotoudeh, Arash Rahmanipour's and many demonstrators' lawyer, will be sentenced on January 9, 2011, to eleven years in jail and barred from practicing law for twenty years for "acting against national security" and "propaganda against the regime."

Creating an atmosphere of terror in this way has been seen to be effective in dissuading protesters from taking to the streets. The Islamic Republic cannot help but dread the thirty-first anniversary of the revolution on February 11, 2010, with opposition forces calling for yet another day of protests.

"*Azizam*, [My darling]," Mandana moans as she hugs her child. "*Koochoolooyeh man* [my little one]. I am so proud of you. You have done what I never dared to do."

"Stop it, Mom," Azadeh laughs. "The entire population was there, and so were you."

Her mother continues to shower her with praise. "My dear child, you were so brave. You have changed the direction in which our country is heading. But now . . . you must leave."

The young woman sits bolt upright. "Are you crazy? Is this a joke?"

"I would die for you, my angel," Mandana smiles, "but just look at what's happening around us. You'll end up in prison. It's only a matter of time. I love you with all my heart, Azi, but you have to leave."

"No way," she interrupts abruptly. "What's wrong with you? After everything that I . . . that *we* have been through? You want me to abandon ship now?"

"No, Azi, no," her mother repeats, kissing her daughter's hair frantically. "Nothing is forever, you know that. You can come back as soon as things settle down."

Understanding exactly what this means, Azadeh pushes her mother away and bursts into tears. "No, Mom, no . . ." she cries like a five-year-old. "I don't want to, not now, not when we're this close to winning . . . I'd rather die. And the rally we've set up for 22 bahman (February 11) in Azadi Square? Have you forgotten that?"

Tears run down Mandana's cheeks as she walks slowly toward her daughter and pulls her close. "I understand, my love. I'm like you too. I think about that rally every day. But you know what goes on in prison. Just look at the state of those poor kids when they come out. Think of those who are still there . . . think of Hengameh. Think of the two poor boys who were hanged. I can't watch that happen to you, Azadeh."

"But, Mom, you know me. I accepted all of these risks when I got involved in activism. My people's future is worth all of those sacrifices. Plus, you know how I am. If they even tried to touch me in prison they'd be sorry."

This last statement provokes a laugh from the girl's mother. "Koreh khar [donkey's tail, a term of endearment], I know. I know, and that's why I'm so proud. But if you won't do it for yourself, then do it for me." Azadeh's face contorts as Mandana continues. "It would kill me, you know that. It would kill me."

Two days later, bad news drops like a bombshell. The police have conducted a sweep of homes belonging to Iranian activists. Nineteen feminists, journalists, and others—all of whom are Azadeh's friends and colleagues—have been arrested.

"Khodaya," Mandana screams. "This is killing me." Fortunately, she still has her daughter, by her side as always.

One week later, it is with heavy hearts that mother and daughter enter Imam Khomeini International Airport. The young woman will be leaving the country legally and heading to Europe, where one of her aunts lives, and Mandana prayed all night long that Azadeh would pass through customs without a hitch. The two women are not the only ones saying their good-byes in the terminal, for this evening the tears of dozens of other youngsters flood the airport as they are torn away from their loved ones and their country. They will soon leave, heading to the far corners of the earth, to start a new life.

"*Khak too sareh Ahmadinejad* (Dirt on your head, Ahmadinejad)," one mother stutters as she tries in vain to hold back her tears. Since the ultraconservative first election four years ago, but particularly since June 2009, tens of thousands of young Iranians have been forced to leave their homeland. Despite her mother's promises, her 110 pounds of luggage is packed full of goodies; she made sure to slip in several pounds of pistachios, melon seeds, dates, and dried herbs (essential for a good *ghormeh sabzi*) so that her baby will want for nothing.

"Passengers are requested to make their way to the boarding lounge."

The time has come. Azadeh, who cannot control her shaking, must go.

"Don't worry," Mandana whispers, "I'll see you very soon, my darling."

The girl stands glued to the spot, in her mother's arms, biting her lips to prevent herself from bursting into tears.

"Mom, please let me stay," she begs. "Prison would be a hundred times better than this hell."

Feeling weak but holding herself together remarkably well, Mandana pushes her daughter toward the shuttle. "I love you, *koochooloo*."

Azadeh bursts into tears but does not look back. An airport security agent suddenly grabs her by the arm. "*Khanoom* (Ma'am). Please, put back your headscarf in the correct manner."

"*Koofteh Jomhouri Eslami*" [Fucking Islamic Republic], she thinks to herself. A few minutes later, Mandana's cell phone vibrates. It is her daughter, reassuring her that she made it through customs without any trouble.

"Thank you, Mom." She sends a kiss down the phone line. "Thank you for everything. See you very soon."

As a short series of beeps signals the end of the call, the phone strikes the airport floor violently: Mandana has fainted.

30

THE ISLAMIC REPUBLIC has been gearing up for this day for the last month and a half. After the unfortunate turn of events on Ashura Day, the republic is celebrating its thirty-first anniversary. To mark the occasion, it has decided to go all out and put on a spread to remember, the party of all parties. The enormous celebration in Azadi Square will take place in the very same spot that saw the triumph of the revolution in 1979. The very same spot where just eight months ago, millions of Iranians demonstrated in silence before being massacred. Of course a big party would not be a big party if it were not attended by huge numbers of guests, with crowds in the thousands if possible.

So, how do you encourage them to come? Do you offer them free entrance to the event? No, that's not quite enough. How about an open bar? Getting there, but even that is not quite enough to pack the place out after eight months of ferocious repression and the murders, arrests, torture, rapes, trials, and executions which came along with it.

Remember to bring all of your friends, family, and neighbors with you; the more the merrier as the saying has it. And the icing on the cake is that you are guaranteed to be on live television. Life is beautiful, what more could you wish for?

Somehow, however, you feel hesitant, unsure of whether you really want to help serve the interests of the Islamic Republic, an institution that you curse every day of your life. Then of course there are the children, who would have no one to look after them. The mullahs have just one thing to say to that: relax, they have thought of everything. There will be free fruit juice for your kids too, and if they behave themselves, they may even get an ice cream. You are probably thinking to yourself that food is not the only important thing in life and, of course, you are quite right. That is why your little ones will be given an opportunity to see all sorts of processions: to watch tanks, horses, and even helicopters. It is better than Disneyland.

Obviously, you begin to have your doubts. "This can't be possible," you tell yourself. "All these treats without asking anything in return?" Life has taught you that nothing in this world is free, but fortunately for you, the mullahs are kind people. They would not dare ask you for even the smallest amount of money, nor would they ask—as they have done a little too much in the past—that you shout slogans on their behalf; they would not want your children to learn any bad words. They will not even insist that your wives wear their strict black chadors; they simply do not care about that stuff today. Gentlemen, you will have a rare chance to admire your dear sisters with their headscarves hanging loose . . . and who knows, if nobody is looking, perhaps you could even reach out a hand in their direction.

No, this year, the one and only demand is this: The dress code states that you must not wear green. "Why not?" you ask yourself. It seems that you are beginning to overthink things. First of all, it is not a nice color, but as you rightly point out, it is still the color of the prophet, the same prophet which the Islamic Republic has been shoving down your throats for the last thirty-one years. Seeing as you are paying such close attention, I will tell you the truth. This color is the rallying cry of a handful of rioters, so-called Iranians whose pockets bulge with American dollars and who want nothing more but to ruin our party. That would be a little cruel, would it not?

These people are hiding behind an election, the presidential election of June 2009 to be precise, using it as a handy excuse. It is all coming back to you now; that was the very same election in which you were forced to vote for Ahmadinejad. That was all for your own good though, as you well know.

Anyway, whether these people are right or not, you know full well that the president—whether he goes by Ahmadinejad, Mousavi, or any other name—does not care two hoots for you. There is no point pretending to get angry, for you must have already known.

And do not worry about these little green men of which we speak; they are just here to shout a few slogans and ruin your party. Whatever happens, you are in good hands and, once again, we have thought of everything. Our agents, either in their Robocop outfits or in plain clothes, will be watching everything from very, very close up.

"Are they armed?" you ask. Why of course they are; it is your safety at stake here. If you are wondering how you can be sure that you yourself will not be targeted, then the answer is simple: you won't be wearing green. One more thing: if you were hoping for exotic dancers, swinging their hips on the podium for your personal enjoyment, then you will be disappointed. Instead, you will have to listen to the speech of a rather unattractive man, not the most stylish around, who will not even have bothered shaving for the occasion. Sorry about that, but it is your dear president himself. Like I said, not everything can be free. The Islamic Republic needs you so that it, in turn, can help you have the happiest day of your life. We will be one gigantic, glorious team but whatever you do, do not forget the number of the coach you came on. It would be a shame if you woke up tomorrow morning to find yourself on the other side of the country, in a strange, foreign village.

"An enormous crowd invaded Tehran's Azadi Square," Iranian television is proud to announce, back on the air after an eight-month absence. Indeed, the entire length of Enghelab Avenue, which leads onto Azadi Square, is lined with dozens of parked, colorful buses. The star of the show—Ahmadinejad himself—begins his speech.

"Iran is now a nuclear state . . . I would like to announce at the top of my voice that the first delivery of uranium enriched to 20 percent has been successfully produced and handed over to scientists."

There is excitement all around, despite the fact that many people did not understand a word of what was said. In the middle of the crowd, Omid is surrounded. He looks around nervously at the thousands of demonstrators encircling him. He knows that he is not alone. The young man wears a green ribbon around his wrist, carefully hidden inside the sleeve of his coat. The protesters glance around fearfully, unsure of when they should show themselves. Without any clear direction from opposition leaders, the young man had instead made the decision to follow the often-risky advice of movement leaders outside the country. Among them is Mohsen Sazegara, founder of the Revolutionary Guard, and film director Mohsen Makhmalbaf. Thanks to satellite television and the Internet, they called their people to action and suggested yet another infiltration of an official gathering. The proposed strategy was to arrive at Azadi Square in the early hours of the morning—all signs of green carefully hidden away—and to slip through the nets cast wide by the impressive number of security forces in attendance. Then, Mahmoud Ahmadinejad's speech in full swing, they were to whip out the colored symbols in front of state television cameras, which had to be broadcasting the president's speech to a live audience. Another suggestion was to dress as a Basiji and beat the militiamen at their own game.

"Well, that sure worked . . . now there's no way of telling who is who." Omid begins to get annoyed, his green ribbon still out of sight. "By playing their game, we've gotten ourselves trapped."

He glances to his left. A large number of militiamen are also present in the crowd, hiding out, chaperoned by the police force who have a greater presence than ever today. The regime supporters are the only ones who do not notice a thing. As was to be expected, they responded in great numbers to the invitation and are now beaming with joy as they wave the miniature Islamic Republic flags or giant portraits of the supreme leader that have just been handed out as gifts. Others chug down the orange juice they were promised as compensation.

"Dirt on their heads," Omid consoles himself.

"*Allahu Akbar*," a muezzin shouts abruptly through a speaker.

"*Allahu Akbar*," the people reply through their beaming smiles.

Feeling isolated in the center of the crowd, Omid does not say a word. His anger is rising. "Assholes. They had no right. No right whatsoever."

As for Kian, he treated himself to a nice lie-in this morning, unlike several of his friends, who left at dawn for a weekend in Shomal. It is already noon when the singer arrives in Enghelab Square, and he is soon disappointed.

"Oh no," he shouts. "Green or no green, it's impossible to get into the square."

This is not because of overcrowding but because, in front of him, he sees a literal wall of special security officers blocking his way. "I've never seen so many cops in my life," he bursts.

Anyone wearing even the slightest hint of green should watch out, for they would be beaten on the spot. This is exactly what happened to one poor young man who naively thought that he could play a game of cat and mouse on this anniversary day. He was quickly caught by two police officers, cornered in an alley, undressed, and strangled before being savagely beaten. Hoping instead for some kind of counterparty—or counterdemonstration, he should say—possibly in Sadeghieh Square, Kian decides to head off in that direction. On the way he notices a crowd gathered around two Thoroughbred Arabian horses on Enghelab Boulevard. In the saddles are two hooded ninjas, dressed in black from head to toe and carrying Iranian flags. Behind them is a tank, behind which a man in a black smoking jacket and mask forces a smile from behind the wheel of his hearse. On the side of the coffin are a pair of American flags, and an undertaker in a *Scream* mask amuses the crowd with his reaper's hook. Entranced, the audience captures the unique moment on their cell phones.

"It's a real carnival they've put on here," Kian moans. "The faster these guys get back to the boonies, the better."

In Hafteh-Tir Square, Javad cannot control his yawning. It is true that there is not a whole lot going on; not a single protester or student to have a pop at. The other difference is that the militiaman is on foot today. Could this be a punishment for his disappointing results in December?

"Today, our Basiji brothers from around the country have been brought in to make sure that nothing goes wrong," he reassures himself. "Each chapter from the provinces has been assigned one of the capital's neighborhoods. I was told to stay in Hafteh-Tir, that's all." The young man has received strict orders. "Crack down on any hostile group comprised of more than two people," he explains as he plays with his rosary beads. "But even that is not necessary today. It seems that the party is already over for some."

From out of nowhere, an elderly lady limps toward him. "Excuse me, young man. Are you a Basiji?"

Javad is taken aback by the question. "Why?" he replies.

Far from put off by the militiaman's cold response, the grandmother asks again, "You are a Basiji, aren't you?"

"Yeah, so what?" he responds dryly. In response, the old lady displays a huge smile.

"From the bottom of my heart, I hope that you will never make the mistake of getting married."

"What?" Javad asks, thrown off guard.

"So that your pitiful race is stamped out *inshallah* once and for all."

"Get out of here, crazy bitch."

Happy as she could possibly be, the old lady limps away as she came in.

Safe in his taxi, Reza scours the capital for clients to pick up *dar bast,* or in other words people who he can drive independently and off the books, making for better pay. Tonight's *ghormeh sabzi* sure will smell good, especially given all of this traffic, which for once is moving easily. But he too will quickly be disappointed, for there are just not many people out on the streets today.

"*Baba,*" he shouts out. "The only people in Tehran tonight are security officers. If only they hadn't been dropped off in buses, I could have made a fortune tonight!" Perhaps he does not know what day it is.

"Of course I do, we've been waiting for this day for two months." So then what is Reza doing here, baking in his taxi, weaving his way through the streets of Tehran?

"Listen, I have to bring food home at night," he offers as justification. "And anyway, you saw what they've been doing to those young kids . . . it's like Russian roulette today!"

Back in Azadi Square, the big celebration is drawing to a close. The crowd is exhausted after a long day, and they head back now to

Enghelab Avenue in smaller groups. Taking advantage of the worn-out police officers, dozens of green protesters finally unveil themselves and begin to chant timidly.

"Death to the dictator."

Once again, they have underestimated the police, and seconds later, tear gas hits them full on in the face. For once these green protesters have turned red, to the great amusement of the countryfolk. The police are in no mood to show mercy today, and it is the leaders of the opposition, all present in the crowd, who will pay the price. Zahra Rahnavard, Mir-Hossein Mousavi's wife, was struck with a violent punch, Mehdi Karoubi fell victim to tear gas, and Ali Karoubi—his youngest son—was arrested and tortured.

"Hijacking their anniversary was a terrible idea," Omid is angry. "Especially after they had a month and a half to prepare. We should have gathered somewhere else."

On his way home, he witnesses a strange scene. It seems that dozens of his fellow men have spotted an opportunity and are turning this event into a flea market, right on the sidewalk itself. For sale there are Iranian pop CDs, American DVDs, even a few pairs of underwear.

"I guess these guys are the winners," Omid laughs, nervously.

Thirty feet on, his laughter suddenly stops as he sees pushing and shoving going on around a kiosk.

"Action, at last," he cries as he rushes towards the crowd.

The demonstrators are fighting . . . over the free sandwiches they were promised. Omid hangs his head. "I feel sorry for my people. Really sorry."

Sounds rise up from beneath Tehran's streets. With no possible way of expressing themselves aboveground in Azadi Square, Kian and his fellow musicians have taken to the capital city's subway instead. In the cars as in the corridors, these Persian cats are finally having their say.

"Oh, treacherous leader, may you be banished from this land. You have ruined our country's soil, you have killed our nation's young people. *Allahu Akbar*. You have wrapped thousands of bodies in your shrouds. *Allahu Akbar*. Death to you. Death to you. Death to you."

Hiding out in a Middle Eastern town, shadowed by the Iranian authorities, Arya has just received his visa for a capital city in the West. In just a few days, he will be in Europe, but this fortunate turn of events does not seem to please him. Far from it in fact, for Arya is devastated, although perhaps not for the reason one might suspect.

"I feel alone here and useless, but I guess that's just life."

The young man already has plans, specifically the creation of an independent media along with his exiled peers, through which they can reach out to the Iranian people.

"We've lost the battle, there's no denying that. But we haven't failed. One year after the coup d'état we were forced to suffer, the Green Movement is still alive and kicking. That is unbelievable in itself, and nothing will ever be the same in Iran. We'll have to think of different ways to proceed, perhaps through strikes or something, but one important thing is to get the entire working class on board. This year, that portion of the population is going to see a crisis the likes of which they've never seen before.

"To those in the West, all I ask is that you do not forget. You must do everything you can to inform people and to keep up the pressure on the Islamic Republic in the area of human rights. We will take care of the rest.

"June 12, 2010, is an important date. It will mark the first anniversary of the birth of our movement's. That day will not mark the anniversary of the Islamic Republic but of *us*. All it will take to make them fall is for a hundred thousand of us to act together. So that Neda, Sohrab, Taraneh, Mohsen, and all of the others whose blood ran in the streets did not die for nothing. Our history is in the making. My people, I love you. *Dametoon garm*."

Endnotes

Chapter 2

[1] Khatami was Iran's reformist president from 1997 to 2005.

Chapter 3

[1] Translator's note: Here the author refers to Lionel Jospin, French Prime Minister from 1997 to 2002. He ran for president in 2002 (for the second time), was eliminated in the first round, and promptly announced his retirement from politics.

[2] Hatamikia is a famous Iranian film maker.

[3] Saeed Mortazavi was nicknamed the "Butcher of the Press."

[4] Near Qom at the center of the country.

[5] The twelfth hidden imam.

[6] Today's figure stands at around one thousand.

Chapter 4

[1] Mousavi refers here to the president's top advisor, Esfandiar Rahim Mashaei.

[2] Ahmadinejad and his government.

[3] Iranian students are subject to a system of stars which can be used to eliminate them from the university system.

[4] The amount of time given to each candidate.

[5] Minister of Education under Khatami and reformist candidate at the 2005 presidential election.

[6] Perhaps a hint of what could be called "Ahmadinejadsim."

Chapter 5

[1] The Paris Techno Parade is an annual parade in the French capital celebrating techno music. With attendance in the hundreds of thousands each year, is one of the largest such events in the world.

Chapter 9

[1] Translator's note: The original French text referred to the party's guests arriving "sans chemise sans pantalon" (literally "without a shirt or pants"), a reference to the pop song of that title made famous in France in the 1970s by Rika Zaraï. The idea behind this expression is that shirts (*chemises*) and pants (*pantalons*) are a sign of social standing and that, when these are left at the door, one can coexist with one's peers more happily.

[2] "May Ali help you"—an expression commonly used when asking for strength from above.

Chapter 11

[1] A reference to the traditional pro-regime demonstrations.

Chapter 12

[1] This phrase is often used in Persian slang to express great admiration for somebody.

Chapter 21

[1] Mosharekat is the name of Mir-Hossein Mousavi's party.

[2] Could this technique be seen as reminiscent of the Ahmadinejad–Mousavi debate?

Chapter 22

[1] This phrase is commonly used in Persian slang to express annoyance at somebody.

Chapter 28

[1] Translator's note: Paolo Maldini is an Italian soccer player, popular among female fans.

THANKS: To the Iranian people, so *bahal,* so proud, so brave. To all of my friends who stayed behind, despite the dangers, and who continue to send me updates on a daily basis. To Farzaneh, Siamak, Ava, Neda, and Rose.

BRADNER LIBRARY
SCHOOLCRAFT COLLEGE
18600 HAGGERTY ROAD
LIVONIA, MICHIGAN 48152